STICK IT TO YOUR TICKET

THE UNOFFICIAL GUIDE TO BEATING
YOUR PARKING TICKET IN CHICAGO

Sheldon Zeiger, JD

Designed and Printed by

Falcon Books
San Ramon, California

Published by
Sheldon Zeiger Publishing
2038 N. Clark St., #135
Chicago, IL 60614

ISBN 978-0-9822346-0-0

PRINTED IN THE UNITED STATES OF AMERICA

Acknowledgements

I want to express my sincere gratitude to all those who helped me complete this project. Special thanks to Joen Kinnan my editor; Jennifer Mau, for her cover design and photography; Ilene Zeiger for her photography of Chicago locations and Ken Debono of Falcon Books for his advice, production design and printing. I especially want to thank all of my colleagues at the City of Chicago, the dedicated hearing officers and employees at the Department of Revenue and the Department of Administrative Hearings.

HOW *NOT* TO USE THIS GUIDE

Unless you want to know more about parking tickets than any sane person should, I would not read this book cover to cover. It is written by someone who for 15 years dedicated his life to parking tickets and is clearly demented. Proceed with caution because you may become an expert in this rather obscure and otherwise irrelevant area of the law. If you decide to read this book in its entirety, you may even be tempted to discuss parking tickets with friends and family. From personal experience I can tell you that this is a mistake. Their response will include a blank expression followed by an automatic physical reaction involving eyes rolling back in their heads. Let it be said that on a scale of 1 to10 of interesting conversation, parking tickets rank somewhere below navel lint. So tread carefully when discussing parking tickets with anyone you care about. Excessive knowledge or wisdom regarding this subject matter may be dangerous to your interpersonal relationships and mental health. Reading this book may not make you the most popular person within your social circle, but it may – over time – save you from inconvenience and from shelling out significant sums of money.

HOW TO USE THIS GUIDE

The purpose of this book is to provide you with a basic understanding of the signs and parking ordinance in Chicago. This information alone will help you avoid the aggravation and expense of unnecessary parking tickets. If you receive a ticket, refer to the Table of Contents for appropriate page numbers. Abstain from the any inclination or urge to offer an excuse as to why you received your ticket. (See chapter 2.) Examine your alleged violation carefully and determine if it is properly written on its face. (See chapter 4.) If any information on the face of the violation is incorrect or missing, contest your ticket. If the ticket is properly written, then read the law regarding the specific ordinance involved. (See chapter 3.) Determine which – if any – of the available defenses or exemptions apply. (See chapter 5.) Do you have an honest basis for contesting your ticket? What evidence do you require to have a reasonable expectation of proving your defense and convincing a hearing officer to dismiss your ticket? (These issues are discussed ad nauseam in chapters 6 and 7.) Finally, prepare diligently for your in-person hearing or your contest by mail and let justice be served Chicago style.

WHAT YOU *DON'T* WANT TO SEE ON YOUR CAR WHEN YOU COME OUT OF YOUR HOME!

WHERE YOU *DON'T* WANT TO VISIT AT 2:00 A.M. ON A SATURDAY NIGHT!

STICK IT TO YOUR TICKET

THE UNOFFICIAL GUIDE ON
HOW TO BEAT A PARKING TICKET IN CHICAGO

TABLE OF CONTENTS

IV. THE PARKING TICKET: PRIMA FACIE CASE 42

V. DEFENSES AND EXEMPTIONS 48

VI. CONTESTING YOUR TICKET 52

CHAPTER ONE

INTRODUCTION

The city of Chicago maintains that the issuance of parking and compliance tickets is tied directly to quality of life issues. It is done to increase public safety and neighborhood stability, to promote the free flow of traffic and to accommodate motorists with special needs. The city assures us that parking tickets make Chicago a great place to live, work and raise a family.

Let me make it clear that I love Chicago. I was born here and grew up on the south side. I wouldn't want to live anywhere else. But excuse me for being cynical. Is it possible that, in addition to the quality of life issues mentioned above, Chicago's Department of Revenue may be equally interested in the $160 million a year, generated from parking violations?

The purpose of this book arises out of a need for citizen education regarding the parking ordinance and ticket enforcement program. Since the current parking program began in September, 1990, the city has provided the public with three pamphlets. In 1990, the city distributed the infamous "Your Ticket to Boot Hill." The pamphlets currently available are titled "Your Guide to Chicago's Ticket Enforcement Program" and "Parking your Motorcycle or Scooter in Chicago." I will not disagree that these pamphlets provide valuable procedural information regarding navigating the system; however, they are wholly inadequate to teach citizens how to avoid parking tickets. Think about this: Here is a public safety program that over seventeen years has generated over a billion dollars, yet the program's entire parking-regulation education budget involves the distribution of three free pamphlets. We must ask ourselves whether the city *really* wants its citizens informed regarding the parking ordinance.

I worked within the parking program for fifteen years from August, 1990 to May, 2005. I worked as both a hearing officer for the Department of Revenue and as an Administrative Law Officer with the Department of Administrative Hearings. During my tenure, I adjudicated over 100,000 parking tickets both in person and by mail. I've heard every excuse imaginable, but I was almost never persuaded to dismiss a ticket. I've also heard every valid defense that allowed me under the law to dismiss thousands of tickets. This book will provide you with all the practical tools you will need to avoid or increase your odds of beating a parking ticket in Chicago

This book will focus entirely on parking tickets. I will not specifically discuss the related issues of towing, booting and drivers' license suspensions. Each of these subjects is related to receiving parking tickets. For example, you will never be towed by the city without an associated parking ticket. Private towing is another matter altogether. A boot requires three or more tickets that have reached final determination or two tickets that doubled and have been outstanding for a year. Drivers' license suspensions result from a whopping ten tickets that have doubled. Let it be said, if you understand the law and signage and you don't ignore your tickets altogether, you will be less likely to have to deal with any of these parking-related nightmares.

The primary objective of this book involves explaining the parking ordinance and describing the signage so that you can avoid the highly unpleasant experience of receiving a parking ticket. By far the best method for beating a parking ticket in Chicago is to understand the law and signage and thereby avoid getting a parking ticket in the first place.

The second objective of this book involves learning how to properly contest a parking ticket. Although there is no guarantee that you will beat every ticket or that you *should* beat every ticket, what I do promise is that by following my advice you will dramatically increase your odds.

I understand that it is often impossible to avoid a ticket. If you drive and park in Chicago, then parking tickets are a likely risk at one time or another. In numerous areas of Chicago there are far too many drivers who have no legal parking options. If you must park – and often you must – you are bound to get a ticket. The city issues several million tickets a year, many of them under these circumstances, so you should feel no shame or stigma upon receiving a parking ticket because everyone gets them.

In fact, the city issues close to 2.8 million parking tickets per year. Of these tickets, approximately 10 percent are contested. Of those tickets that are contested, almost 53 percent are dismissed. That leaves 47 percent of the contested tickets – remember only 10 percent are contested – that must be paid. Every citizen has the right to contest every parking ticket. I'm a rationalist, and I believe that citizens should be contesting a large percentage of the approximately 2.5 million tickets that are paid without contesting. Why would you voluntarily give your hard-earned money to the city when you have the right to contest?

Think about it. If you own a car and you drive and park in Chicago, you'll be glad you bought this book. If I can help you avoid or beat a single ticket then this book will be worth many times what you paid for it.

GOALS:

UNDERSTAND THE PARKING ORDINANCE AND SIGNAGE SO AS TO AVOID EVER RECEIVING A TICKET.

IF YOU RECEIVE A TICKET, LEARN TO PRESENT A VALID DEFENSE AND THEREBY CONVINCE A HEARING OFFICER TO DISMISS YOUR TICKET.

CHAPTER TWO

WHY EXCUSES NEVER WORK

My editor wants me to bury this chapter way in the back of this guide book. She asked me, why I want to put the excuses chapter up front? She maintains, why not just get on with teaching how to really beat a parking ticket?

Let me try to explain….

During the many years that I worked for the city as an ALO, when ever I was in a social setting a friend or family member would always ask me about their most recent parking ticket. They couldn't help themselves. They had to know my opinion about whether they could get out of their ticket. They would tell me their story which usually involved 3-5 minutes of mind numbing narrative explaining the unfortunate series of events that led up to their meter or rush hour violation.

I would listen intently. When they stopped for a breath or finished their story, which ever came first, I would tell them that I truly sympathized with their situation. However, so far nothing that they've told me would help them get out of their ticket. It was at this point that things would usually start getting ugly. In an instant, aunt Edith's warm chubby face would turn icy, her otherwise sweet disposition turned sour and with an annoyed, approaching angry tone in her voice she would attack. "What do you mean, my story doesn't matter? I'm telling you the truth. Why don't you believe me? What is the matter with you? Are you heartless? Why did I bother asking a lawyer for his opinion in the first place? You never let anyone out of their ticket do you? You can't beat city hall. I'm moving to Arizona. Why didn't you become something useful, a dermatologist like your cousin Elliot?"

While physically backing away, I would offer to pay her ticket for her. I almost felt as if it was my fault for being part of the system. I would try and explain, "Of course I believe you. You're my aunt. Why would you lie to me? But your story, your reasons, your excuses, standing alone will never get you out of your parking ticket."

In various forms, this scenario was repeated hundreds of times with family, friends and acquaintances. For 15 years, I was afraid to go to a party or for that matter my parents house for the holidays. If I could tell the general public, the world, one thing about parking tickets it would be that excuses don't work.

A parking ticket imposes a civil sanction (a fine) for an unlawful act (an alleged parking violation) without requiring a showing of intent [to commit the unlawful act] by the responsible party (the registered owner of the vehicle). For these purposes, the parking law is a strict liability ordinance. In other words, your state of mind at the time of the ticket is not necessarily relevant in determining whether you're responsible to pay for the ticket. The reason that you parked where you did might provide context but is otherwise unrelated to your defense. However, that does not prevent citizens from telling some pretty fanciful tales to get off the hook.

As a hearing officer, I always assumed that a citizen was telling me the truth. But, even if I was told the most convincing story, and I was sympathetic to the citizen's circumstance, I still required a valid defense to dismiss the ticket. Your nonfiction scenario may provide endless entertainment for the ALOs as they pass around your story. You may even engender sympathy if the hearing officer is still capable of this emotion after years of listening to every conceivable and inconceivable situation. You may have done nothing wrong, and your excuse may be entirely factual. That doesn't matter. Under the parking law your reasons and your excuse, standing alone, will not beat a ticket.

Let me give you a sampling of the various excuses a hearing officer confronts on a daily basis. I want to give you some idea of what things people are willing to say to try to get out of a ticket. I also want to comment on why these excuses never work.

- The officer was rude. (I would apologize for the officer's rude conduct before finding the citizen liable for the ticket.)

- The officer was a racist (same as above).

- The officer could have asked me to move. (He didn't. Instead he wrote a ticket.)

- The officer had a quota. (The issue is irrelevant. The city denies that there are quotas. However, police officers and parking enforcement aides are required to write thousands of tickets per day.)

- The doorman or security guard said it was all right to park here. (Unless the doorman protects your vehicle from an officer writing a ticket, it's still a good ticket. A valid exemption exists where a police officer directs you to park at the location of the ticket.)

- I have a constitutional right to park on the street. (Of course you have a right to park on the public way, but the city also has the right to issue you a parking ticket.)

- I wasn't parked at 242 S. Kedzie. I was parked at 221 S. Kedzie. (Where your car is parked doesn't have an address; only a building has an address. All an officer is required to do is give a reasonable approximation of where you were parked. Note, however, that a wrong block or street *is* a bad address and a valid reason to contest for no proper location or invalid prima facie case.)

- I received a rush hour ticket at 8:59 a.m. and the ticket says 9:01 a.m. (Whose watch or clock is correct? Yours or the officer's? What proof do you have that your time was correct? Your radio? The U.S. Naval Observatory Master Clock Time?)

- Why me? No one else got a ticket. (Thousands of vehicles are ticketed every day.)

- There was no ticket on my car. (Even though the ordinance requires delivery of the ticket in person or on the car, DOAH policy maintains that notice by mail meets this delivery requirement.)

- I live outside of Chicago and didn't know about the parking law. (Ignorance of the law is never a defense for a parking ticket.)

- I just parked there for one minute. (Wrong place at the wrong time)

- My business meeting or doctors visit went too long. (Pay your ticket.)

- I was out of town on business (or on vacation) and I didn't know about the street cleaning (or other temporary) signs. (If you leave your car parked on the public way, it is subject to any temporary signs posted even if you're in Florida.)

- I pay my taxes to park on the street. (You pay your taxes to repair and maintain the street so that you *can* park.)

- I only parked an inch beyond the sign. (If any portion of your vehicle – even the bumper – is beyond the sign, it is enough to get a ticket.)

- The sign was hidden on the other side of the tree or truck. (Did you look on the other side of the tree or truck where you parked?)

- There is only one sign on the block. (Depending on violation, it may be that only one sign is required. Check corner to corner.)

- There was no sign marking the alley, driveway, hydrant, handicapped curb cut, crosswalk, or area under the fire escape or theater entrance. (A sign isn't necessary because these violations speak for themselves.)

- Where there was a street-cleaning sign: I parked after street cleaning occurred or the street was not cleaned. (Unless a temporary sign was removed, these signs read 9 a.m. to 3 p.m.)

- I have a good parking record. (You used to have a good parking record. You do not get graded on your parking record.)

- I received my ticket while volunteering or doing charity work. (Good people get tickets too. Bad tickets sometimes happen to good people.)

- I received my ticket while in church/synagogue/mosque services. (Somehow using your religion as an excuse for a parking ticket seemed sacrilegious. Most hearing officers are atheists when it comes to parking tickets.)

- I'm begging for mercy/have no job/give me a break. (I feel your pain; pay your ticket.)

- Make a scene by crying, ranting and raving. (I would try to calm the citizen down before finding him or her liable and calling for a security guard.)

- My car was booted when I got this ticket. (You can get a ticket when your car is booted).

- I went inside the store to get quarters to feed the meter. (Always carry quarters in your car.)

- I paid for the meter during rush hour. (You can still get a rush-hour ticket.)

- I received two tickets for two different violations at the same time and place. (The largest number of tickets I ever saw in one spot was five for different compliance violations.)

- I had a grace period because my flashers were on. (If you are not parked in a loading zone that requires flashers or double parked in traffic where there are safety concerns, do not put your flashers on. The officer isn't saying to himself, "I'll give this guy a pass because he's only going to be parked illegally for a few minutes." Flashers attract officers to write tickets because only illegally parked cars put their flashers on.)

- I'm elderly and/or disabled (or my passengers are). (This creates sympathy, but the hearing officer will still need a valid defense to dismiss the ticket.)

- I was giving birth. (No medical emergency defense. Try bringing in both the infant and a birth certificate.)

- I have a urinary tract infection and had to go to the bathroom. (There is no medical emergency or illness defense.)

- I had an allergic reaction. My tongue bloated, and I couldn't breathe. (Same as above. A parking ticket is a small price to pay for being alive.)

- My car broke down or ran out of gas. (Not a vehicle emergency defense for a ticket. It is an emergency defense only for parking on a parkway.)

- I had to park to save my sick or dying pet puppy, bunny or kitten. (PETA member pulled over to save a pigeon.)

- The weather was terrible. These are excuses for snow, wind, fog or rain. (This *is* Chicago in the winter)

- There was a school emergency. (Somehow using your children to get out of a ticket just doesn't seem right.)

- I had to go to a wedding, graduation, anniversary or funeral. (Remember death is not a defense for a parking ticket in Chicago.)

- (From a woman:) I had to park here. This is a dangerous neighborhood at night. (Safety first always, but this is not a defense.)

EXCUSES THAT WERE SO OUTRAGEOUS I DIDN'T KNOW HOW TO RESPOND:

- The officer tried to pick me up. When I said no, he wrote a ticket.

- Heart bypass patient who lifted up his shirt to show me his scars from surgery.

- Citizen claimed pre senile dementia. (Mental illness is not a defense to a parking ticket. Insanity defense rarely works in a criminal case.)

- Citizen wrote that he couldn't get to his car before rush hour because he had to service his girlfriend or she'd break up with him.

- A citizen informed me in an in-person hearing that his daughter had her first menstrual period in his new Jaguar, and he had to park to clean up the car. (No mention of taking care of his daughter.)

I understand that living in a crowded city like Chicago subjects us all to certain pressures, abuse and indignities. Some people simply go over the edge when they get a parking ticket. No matter how badly you want to tell the ALO your life story, exercise self-control. It's fine to give context to your defense, but you need to be credible in order to convince the hearing officer to dismiss your ticket. **THE HEARING OFFICER MUST BELIEVE YOUR DEFENSE, NOT YOUR STORY.** When you rely exclusively on *why* you parked, you lose credibility. When a hearing officer hears or reads your excuse, he or she will appear to be listening intently, sympathizing with your plight. In reality, the officer is probably already typing in a "liable" decision. Give yourself the opportunity to beat the ticket. Help the ALO help you. Give the officer something to hang a hat on so he or she can dismiss your ticket. Give the officer a real defense.

LESSON: MINIMIZE YOUR EXCUSES AND FOCUS ON YOUR DEFENSE.

CHAPTER THREE

VIOLATIONS: PARKING ORDINANCE AND SIGNAGE

Since it is always better not to get a parking ticket in the first place, you can save yourself time, money and hassle if you are familiar with Chicago's parking ordinance and signage. Understanding the city's parking regulations may also help you in your defense should you get a ticket. The city's code is detailed below.

Disclaimer: This Code of Ordinances that appear in this book may not reflect the most current legislation adopted by the Municipality. Fine amounts are also subject to change by the Chicago City Council. (Current List of Fines in Appendix)

Section 9-64-020   Parallel parking – Obstruction of traffic.

(a) It shall be unlawful to stand or park any vehicle in a roadway other than parallel with the edge of the roadway headed in the direction of lawful traffic movement and with the curbside wheels of the vehicle within 12 inches of the curb or edge of the roadway; provided however, this prohibition shall not apply to motorcycles or motor scooters, which may be parked diagonally, or to the parking of any vehicle in a designated diagonal parking zone or space.

(b) It shall be unlawful to stand or park any vehicle upon any street in such a manner or under such conditions as to leave available less than 18 feet of the width of the roadway for free movement of vehicular traffic on a two-way street or less than 10 feet of the width of the roadway for free movement of vehicular traffic on a one-way street.

- NOTE: no signs are required.
- Park on the correct side of the street facing traffic flow.
- Park within 12 inches of the curb when parallel parking.
- Motorcycles and scooters are exempt.
- Leave 18 feet for traffic on a two-way street.
- Leave 10 feet for traffic on a one-way street.

Section 9-64-030   Diagonal parking zones.

(a) The commissioner of transportation is hereby authorized to establish diagonal parking zones and to designate such zones by placing and maintaining suitable signs and markings.

(b) It shall be unlawful to park any vehicle in any designated diagonal parking zone or space except diagonally to the edge of the roadway and within the pavement markings.

  • NOTE: no signs are required.
  • There must be ground markings for a violation to exist.
  • Park within diagonal marking.
  • If you get a ticket, take pictures of where the car was parked and any marking on the ground.

Section 9-64-040 Street cleaning.

(a) For the purpose of facilitating the cleaning of streets, the commissioner of streets and sanitation is authorized to post temporary signs, and the commissioner of transportation to erect and maintain permanent signs designating the day or days of the week and hours of the day and the part of the street or streets in which the parking of vehicles is prohibited because of street cleaning and to further designate such street or streets as "tow zones."

(b) It shall be unlawful to park any vehicle on any street in violation of a sign posted, erected or maintained pursuant to this section.

(c) The commissioner of streets and sanitation is authorized to tow any vehicle parked in violation of this section to the nearest lawful parking space or to move the vehicle temporarily during street cleaning operations.

- Signs required: Tow Zone during Street Cleaning Hours.

- Temporary signs are posted in the afternoon on the day prior to cleaning. Signs state 9 a.m. - 3 p.m. on the day of cleaning.

- There are permanent signs on certain business streets.

- Don't park in violation of signs even after street cleaning has occurred.

- Don't park in violation of signs even if no street cleaning has occurred.

- Missing or obscured signs are a defense.

- If you get a ticket, take pictures corner to corner on the block.

Section 9-64-050 Parking restrictions-Parking for persons with disabilities.

It shall be unlawful to park any vehicle in any space designated by signage as a person with a disability parking space or in any parking stall of a private or public parking lot designated by the lot owner or his agent as reserved for person with a disability parking unless the vehicle bears person with a disability or disabled veteran state registration plates or a person with a disability parking decal or device issued pursuant to…and such vehicle is operated by the person to whom the special registration plates, special decal or device was issued or a qualified operator acting under his express direction while the person with a disability is present.

- Signs required: "Handicapped Spaces Found in Public Lots and Residential Streets."

- In a public lot, the handicapped spot will have markings on the ground and signs posted.

- On a residential street, if the handicapped space is marked, the ordinance will be enforced even if the handicapped person doesn't live there anymore.

- If you get a ticket, a defense is having a properly displayed handicapped placard or plates. On a residential street, your placard or plate number must match that particular spot.

- If you get a ticket, a defense is improperly displayed signs or ground markings.

- If you get a ticket, take pictures of the signage and make copies of your handicap placard. Always maintain proper display of the placard in your defense.

Section 9-64-060   Snow removal.

(a) For the purpose of facilitating snow removal, the commissioner of transportation is authorized to erect and maintain signs prohibiting the parking of vehicles on any street or streets within the city between the hours of 3:00 a.m. and 7:00 a.m. from December 1 of any year to March 31 of the following year and to further designate such street or streets as "tow zones."

(b) It shall be unlawful to park any vehicle on any street in violation of a sign erected or maintained pursuant to this section.

- Signs are required on the entire block.

- A permanent snow removal sign will not only get you a ticket but you will also be towed.

- There may be permanent snow removal signs from 3 a.m. - 7 a.m. from December 1 - March 31.

- If you get a ticket, take pictures of signs from corner to corner.

Section 9-64-070   Parking on snow routes.

It shall be unlawful to park any vehicle for a period of time longer than three minutes for the loading and unloading of passengers or 30 minutes for the loading, unloading, pick-up or delivery of materials from commercial vehicles, whether such location has been designated as a loading zone or not, on any street that has been designated by appropriate signs as a "Snow Route" at any time the snow on the street exceeds two inches in depth and until the snow stops falling and for the necessary period of time until all snow removal operations have been completed.

- Signs are required on the entire block.

- Ordinance will be in effect when snow is in excess of two inches or more on the street.

- Don't park until snow removal has been completed.

- If you get a ticket, taking three minutes to unload passengers is a defense

- If you get a ticket, taking 30 minutes for commercial pickup or delivery is a defense.

- If you get a ticket, take pictures of signs from corner to corner.

Section 9-64-080   Parking restricted on certain days or hours.

(a) The commissioner of transportation is authorized based on traffic need supported by an engineering study, to erect and maintain on any through street or street on which a bus line is operated, appropriate signs indicating no parking between designated hours on either side of the street Monday through Friday.

(b) The commissioner of transportation is authorized to determine, subject to the approval of the city council, those streets or parts of streets upon which standing or parking shall be prohibited within certain hours or permitted for a limited time and to erect and maintain appropriate signs giving notice to the restrictions…at which full time standing or parking restrictions shall be modified to limit the prohibition on standing or parking to Mondays through Fridays or Mondays through Saturdays and to erect and maintain appropriate signs giving notice of the restrictions.

(c) It shall be unlawful to stand or park any vehicle in violation of a sign erected or maintained pursuant to this section.

- Signs are required.

- Rush hour signs from 7 a.m. - 9 a.m. and 4 p.m. - 6 p.m. Monday-Friday may be posted.

- If you get a ticket, take pictures from corner to corner.

Section 9-64-090   Residential permit parking.

(a) When official signs are erected indicating resident permit parking only, parking shall be restricted to service and delivery vehicles whose operators are doing business with residents of the residential permit parking zone and to vehicles displaying resident or visitor parking permits issued pursuant to Section 9-68-020 herein. In addition, a vehicle not in these two categories may park legally for up to 15 minutes in a 24-hour period in a residential permit parking zone if its hazard indicator lights are flashing.

(b) It shall be unlawful to park any unauthorized vehicle in violation of signs erected or maintained pursuant to this section or any other ordinance or city council order which establishes and defines a residential permit order zone for which permits are issued pursuant…

- Signs are required.

- Visitor parking permits issued … herein shall be valid for a 24-hour period from the time of posting.

- Park if you have a permanent or temporary permit properly displayed.

- You have 15 minutes (with your flashers on) to obtain a temporary permit.

- Permit must be properly filled out and displayed on the lower right of windshield on the passenger side.

- Temporary permits are valid for 24 hours from the time of posting for service or delivery vehicles doing business.

- If you get a ticket, take pictures of signs corner to corner.

- If you get a ticket, make a copy of the temporary permit filled out in ink with tape removed.

Section 9-64-100 Parking prohibited.

It shall be unlawful to park any vehicle in any of the following places:

(a) Within 15 feet of a fire hydrant.

(b) In a fire lane.

(c) At any place where the vehicle will block vehicular access to or use of a driveway, alley or fire lane.

(d) At any place where the vehicle will block the use of a curb cut access for handicapped pedestrians.

(e) Under the lowest portion of any fire escape.

(f) Within 20 feet of a crosswalk where official signs are posted.

(g) Within 30 feet of an official traffic signal or stop sign on the approaching side.

(h) On the same side of the public way in front of any entrance or exit of any theater building as defined…

- No signs are required. These violations speak for themselves.

- If you get a ticket, take pictures of the entire area.

- Standing at the location is a defense. (See definitions in appendix of what constitutes lawful standing.)

Section 9-64-110   Parking prohibited.

It shall be unlawful to stand or park any vehicle in any of the following places:

(a) On the roadway side of any vehicle stopped or parked at the edge or curb of a street (double parking).

(b) Within an intersection, except on the continuous side of a "T" intersection.

(c) On a crosswalk.

(d) On a sidewalk.

(e) On a parkway, except in case of an emergency.

(f) Upon any bridge, except those located on North Stockton Drive between North Avenue and Diversey Parkway.

(g) In a viaduct or underpass.

(h) On any railroad tracks or within a distance of 10 feet from the outer rails thereof.

- No signs are required. These violations speak for themselves.

- If you get a ticket, take pictures of the entire area.

Section 9-64-120   Parking on city property.

It shall be unlawful to park any vehicle upon any property owned by the city and used for the transaction of public business where such parking is prohibited by order of the custodian of the property; provided, this section shall not apply to city owned vehicles or to other vehicles whose operation is useful or essential to the proper functioning of the department, board or commission occupying the property. The custodian of the property shall post "No Parking" signs indicating the foregoing prohibition.

It shall be unlawful to stand or park any vehicle upon the premises of a Chicago Housing Authority Development except in such areas designated by official signs or other markings as parking lots.

- Signs are required on city property.

Section 9-64-130   Parking in alleys.

(a) It shall be unlawful to park any vehicle in any alley for a period of time longer than is necessary for the expeditious loading, unloading, pick-up or delivery of materials from such vehicle.

(b) It shall be unlawful to park a vehicle in an alley in such a manner or under such conditions as to leave available less than 10 feet of the width of the roadway for the free movement of vehicular traffic or to block the entrance to any abutting property.

- No signs are required in an alley.

- Expeditious loading or unloading of passengers is allowed.

- Expeditious loading or unloading, pick up or delivery of materials from a vehicle is allowed.

- Don't block the alley; leave 10 feet for traffic.

Section 9-64-140 Common-carrier vehicle stops and stands.

(a) The commissioner of transportation is authorized to establish bus stops upon 20-day prior notice to the alderman of the ward in which the bus stop is located and, subject to the approval of the city council, is authorized to establish horse-drawn carriage stands, bus stands, taxicab stands and stands for other passenger common-carrier motor vehicles on such public streets.

(b) It shall be unlawful to stand or park a vehicle, other than the type of vehicle for which the stop or stand is reserved, in violation of signs posted, in any stop or stand described in subsection (a) that has been officially designated by appropriate signs or markings; provided, however, that this provision shall not apply to a vehicle engaged in the expeditious loading, or unloading of passengers when such standing does not interfere with any bus, horse-drawn carriage or taxicab waiting to enter or about to enter such zone.

- Signs are required.

- Expeditious loading or unloading of passengers is allowed in bus, taxi or carriage stands.

- Don't interfere with use of area.

- If you get a ticket, take pictures of the area and any signage.

Section 9-64-150   Parking prohibited-Fire stations, railroad crossings and hazardous locations.

(a) The commissioner of transportation is authorized to erect and maintain signs indicating no parking at any place within 20 feet of the entrance to any fire station, on the side of any street opposite the entrance to any fire station within 75 feet of the entrance or within 50 feet of the nearest rail or railroad crossing.

(b) The commissioner of transportation is authorized to determine places in which the standing or parking of vehicles would create an especially hazardous condition or would cause unusual delay to traffic and those streets or parts of streets upon which parking shall be prohibited, and to erect and maintain appropriate signs giving notice that standing or parking is prohibited.

(c) It shall be unlawful to stand or park any vehicle in violation of any sign erected or maintained pursuant to this section.

- Signs are required.
- There is no standing or parking any time in tow zones.
- If you get a ticket, take pictures of the entire area.

Section 9-64-160   Curb loading zones.

(a) The commissioner of transportation is authorized subject the approval of the city council, to determine the location of curb loading zones and shall place and maintain appropriate signs indicating the zones and the hours during which standing or parking is restricted.

(b) It shall be unlawful to park any vehicle in any place designated as a curb loading zone during the days of the week or hours of the day when the restrictions applicable to such zones are in effect, except for the expeditious loading and pick-up or unloading and delivery of materials from commercial vehicles and then for a period not to exceed 30 minutes; provided however the operator of a motor vehicle of the first division may stand in a curb loading zone for the purpose of and while actually engaged in the expeditious loading or unloading of passengers when such standing does not interfere with any vehicle used for the transportation of materials which is waiting to enter or about to enter such zone.

- Signs are required.

- Every loading zone sign may have different times, days and restrictions.

- Expeditious loading or unloading of commercial vehicles for 30 minutes is allowed.

- Loading or unloading of passengers is permitted as long as you don't interfere with commercial vehicles or usage.

- For defense purposes if you get a ticket, the driver must have been in the vicinity of the vehicle.

- If you get a ticket, take pictures of area.

- If you get a ticket, provide a receipt from the store whose loading zone was involved at the time of the violation.

Section 9-64-170   Large vehicles-Parking restricted.

(a) It shall be unlawful to park any truck, tractor, semitrailer, trailer, recreational vehicle more than 22 feet in length, self-contained motor home, bus, taxicab or livery vehicle on any residential street for a longer period than is necessary for the reasonably expeditious loading or unloading of such vehicle, except that a driver of a bus may park the bus in a designated bus stand as authorized elsewhere in the traffic code.

(b) It shall be unlawful to park any truck, tractor, semitrailer, trailer or self-contained motor home, or bus on any business street in the city for a longer period than is necessary for the reasonably expeditious loading or unloading of such vehicle, except that a driver of a bus may park the bus in a designated bus stand as authorized elsewhere in the traffic code. It shall be unlawful to park any taxicab on any business street in the city for a period longer than two hours between the hours of 2:00 a.m. and 7:00 a.m.; provided that this prohibition shall not apply to taxi cabs parked on business streets in the 46th ward.

(c) It shall be unlawful to stand or park any vehicle six feet or greater in height within 20 feet of a crosswalk.

(d) A violator of subsection (a) or (b) of this section shall be subject to a fine of $500.00 if the vehicle involved in the violation is a truck tractor, a semitrailer or trailer. In addition to such fine, the truck tractor, semi-trailer or trailer shall be subject to immobilization and impoundment.

- NOTE: No signs are required.

- This provision applies to taxis and livery vehicles on residential streets.

- This provision applies to taxis during the hours of 2 a.m. - 7 a.m. on *any* street.

- This provision applies to vehicles 6 feet in height or taller within 20 feet of a crosswalk.

- This provision refers to the ticketing and booting of trucks and semitrailers on city streets.

Section 9-64-180   Restricted parking – Central business district

(a) Except as provided in subsection (b), it is unlawful to park any vehicle at any time on the following streets: Garvey Court, from Lake Street to Wacker Drive; State Street and Michigan Avenue, from Wacker Drive to Congress Parkway. Except as provided in subsection (b), it is unlawful to park any vehicle during the hours of 6:00 a.m. to 6:00 p.m., Monday through Friday, except for days established as holidays in Section 9-64-010 on any of the following streets: Washington Street, Madison Street and Monroe Street, between State Street and Michigan Avenue; Adams Street and Jackson Boulevard, between Canal Street and Michigan Avenue; Dearborn Street, Clark Street and LaSalle Street, between Washington Street and Jackson Boulevard; and Wacker Drive, from Franklin Street to Van Buren Street.

(b) The restrictions in this section shall not apply in any designated handicapped parking area or to any ambulance, any emergency vehicle owned by a governmental agency, any vehicle owned by a public utility while the operator of the vehicle is engaged in the performance of emergency duties, any taxicab at an officially designated taxicab stand and/or engaged in the expeditious loading or unloading of passengers with disabilities, any passenger vehicle engaged for not more than three minutes in the loading or unloading of passengers, or to the parking of any commercial vehicle engaged in the expeditious loading, unloading, pick-up or delivery of materials in a designated loading zone, or to any bus at a designated bus stop or bus stand…the more restrictive regulations shall apply.

(c) No parking meters shall be installed on those portions of streets listed in subsection (a) where parking is prohibited at all times.

- Signs are required.

Section 9-64-190   Parking meter zones-Regulations.

(a) It shall be unlawful to park any vehicle in a designated parking meter zone or space without depositing United States currency of the denomination indicated on the meter and putting the meter in operation or otherwise legally activating the meter, and, if the meter is of the type that issues a ticket or other token, displaying in the vehicle a ticket or token issued by the meter, or to park any vehicle in such zone or space for a period longer than is designated on or by the meter for the value of the coin or coins deposited in the meter, or the value otherwise registered by the meter.

Upon the expiration of the time thus designated upon or by the meter, the operator of the motor vehicle shall then immediately remove such vehicle from the parking meter zone. No operator of any motor vehicle shall permit such vehicle to remain in the parking meter zone for an additional consecutive time period. These provisions shall not apply during such hours of the day as designated from time to time by order of the city council or on days established as holidays in Section 9-4-010.

(b) Any person who violates or fails to comply with the provisions of subsection (a) of this section while parked in a parking meter zone situated within the area bounded by a line as follows: beginning at the easternmost point of Division Street extended to Lake Michigan; then west on Division Street to LaSalle Street; then south on LaSalle Street to Chicago Avenue; then west on Chicago Avenue to Halsted Street; then south on Halsted Street to Roosevelt Road; then east on Roosevelt Road to its easternmost point extended to Lake Michigan, including parking meter zones on both sides of the above-mentioned streets, shall be subject to the penalty imposed.

- NOTE: Instructions are on the meters, not on signs.

- Be alert for double-bay meters (meters that apply to the parking spots on both sides of the meter) and meter boxes.

- Feed the meter and/or display the paid receipt on the windshield.

- You shouldn't re-feed a meter. (It is not your spot for the entire day.)

- Be aware that you can receive a ticket at a two-hour meter every two hours.

- Read the informational sticker on the front of the meter.

- Watch for Sunday meters on some business streets.

- Parking holidays exempt you from paying the meter. (These parking holidays are listed in the Appendix.)

- To avoid a ticket, if the meter is broken, notify the city. Call (312)-744-PARK and report the broken meter on the day of the violation.

- If you get a ticket (and didn't report the broken meter), write down the meter number and give specific details of the manner in which the meter malfunctioned, i.e., the time was inaccurate after you inserted the money, the coin stuck, etc.

Section 9-64-200   Parking meters-Installation and pavement markings.

(a) The commissioner of transportation shall cause parking meters to be installed in parking meter zones in such numbers, during such hours of operation, at such rates, and at such places as established by the city council and shall have markings painted or placed upon the pavement adjacent to each parking meter, where such markings are appropriate for the type of parking meter installed, for the purpose of designating the parking space for which the meter is to be used. The commissioner shall consult with the parking administrator in determining the number of meters necessary in any zone.

(b) It shall be unlawful to park any vehicle in any designated parking meter space except entirely within the area defined by the markings for that space.

- NOTE: No signs are required.

- The law requires markings on the pavement to designate meter locations.

- If you get a ticket, take pictures of the location.

COMMON COMPLIANCE ISSUES

When an officer writes a ticket for a parking violation, he or she has an opportunity to look your vehicle over carefully. If the vehicle fails to comply with other provisions of the code, you may find to your dismay that you have received one or more tickets for compliance violations as well as the parking violation. Listed below are some of the most common code requirements that could result in compliance violations.

Section 9-40-060 Driving, standing or parking on bicycle paths or lanes prohibited.

The driver of a vehicle shall not drive, unless entering or exiting a legal parking space, or stand, or park the vehicle upon any on-street path or lane designated by official signs or markings for the use of bicycles, or otherwise drive or place the vehicle in such a manner as to impede bicycle traffic on such path or lane. Any person who violates this section shall be fined $100.00 for each offense. Any vehicle parked in violation of this section shall be subject to an immediate tow and removal to a city vehicle pound or authorized garage.

- Signs are required.

9-40-260 Use of Mobile Telephones

(a) Except as provided by subsection (b) of this section, no person shall drive a motor vehicle while using mobile, cellular, analog wireless or digital telephone.

(b) The provisions of the ordinance shall not apply to:

    (1) Law enforcement officers and operators of emergency vehicles when on duty and acting in their official capacities.

    (2) Persons using a telephone with a "hands free" device allowing the driver to talk into and listen to the other party without the use of hands.

    (3) Persons using a telephone to call 911 telephone numbers or other emergency telephone numbers to contact public safety forces.

    (4) Person using a telephone while maintaining a motor vehicle in a stationary parked position and not in gear.

- (c) Any person who violates subsection (a) of this section shall be subject to a fine of $75.00 provided however that if a violation occurs at the time of a traffic accident, the driver may be subject to an additional fine not to exceed $200.00.

Section 9-76-150 Burglar Alarms.

(a) In any vehicle equipped with a continuous or intermittent audible signal device which acts as a burglar alarm, such device shall be limited in operation to four minutes after activation and shall be incapable of further operation until reset to become active again.

(b) No person shall install or maintain in any vehicle registered in the city any continuous or intermittent audible signal device for use as a burglar alarm unless the device is equipped with an automatic shut-off mechanism to terminate the alarm sound after four minutes and an automatic reset mechanism to reengage the alarm for further operation.

(c) Any person who violates this section shall be subject to a fine of $50.00 for each offense. Second violation is $75.00 and all subsequent violation is $100.00. Each installation and each use of an alarm in violation of this section shall constitute a separate and distinct offense; provided, however, it shall not be a violation of this section to operate a device for a period of time in excess of four minutes if the device is designed to be triggered by the unauthorized opening of the hood, trunk or door of the vehicle, or by the breaking of a window, and the operation of the device in excess of four minutes was so caused. A violation of this section on a roadway is hereby declared a public nuisance which may be abated by removing such vehicle pound or authorized garage.

- Show proof that your vehicle was damaged or broken into (police report).
- Show maintenance records from a mechanic showing the alarm was in proper working order.

Section 9-76-160 Registration Plates

(a) Registration plates issued for a motor vehicle other than a motorcycle, trailer, semi-trailer or truck-tractor shall be attached to the front and rear of the vehicle.

(b) The registration plate issued for a motorcycle, trailer or semi-trailer shall be attached to the rear thereof.

(c) The registration plate issued for a truck-tractor shall be attached to the front thereof.

(d) Every registration plate shall at all times be securely fastened in a horizontal position to the vehicle for which it is issued so as to prevent the plate from swinging and at a height o not less than 12 inches from the ground, measuring from the bottom of such plate, in a place and position to be clearly visible and shall be maintained free from foreign materials and in a condition to be clearly legible. No registration plate shall be covered by any tinted or colored screen.

(e) It is illegal to park a vehicle on any roadway if the registration plate or other registration material fails to comply with subsections (a) – (d) of this section.

(f) Every registration plate, temporary permit or evidence of temporary registration must bear evidence of proper registration for the current period and be displayed in the manner required by the secretary of state.

- Don't place your registration plates in the front or rear window. This is an invitation for a ticket. The officer doesn't even need to look down to observe the violation.

Section 9-76-170 City Vehicle Tax Sticker (City Sticker)

The city vehicle tax sticker, for any vehicle requiring a license pursuant to Chapter 3-56 of this code, shall be displayed, and placed and positioned to be clearly visible and maintained in a clearly legible condition and shall be placed on the front windshield in the lower right-hand corner farthest removed from the driver's position approximately one inch from the right and lower edge of the windshield.

- Display your city sticker.

- If you don't have a city sticker and you live in Chicago, buy one!

- As the registered owner of the vehicle, you have a valid defense to a city sticker violation if you have lived in the city for less than 30 days at the time of the violation

- or you have owned the cited vehicle for less than 30 days at time of violation. To get the exemption, buy the sticker and display it. You will need the receipt of purchase and a picture of the display as proof.

- If you receive a compliance violation for failing to display a city sticker and you are not a resident of Chicago, you will need two or more of the following to prove non-city residence:

1. Lease or mortgage agreement showing proof of residency. The issuance dates of the tickets must fall within the term of the lease.

2. A receipt for, or a comparable sticker, issued by a municipality or township other than the city of Chicago.

3. Utility bills showing your address, when the issuance dates of the tickets fall within the service period.

Section 9-76-180 Safety Belts

(a) Each driver and front seat passenger of a passenger motor vehicle shall wear properly adjusted and fastened seat safety belts, except that a child less than six years of age shall be protected as required by the Child Passenger Protection Act of the State of Illinois. Each driver of a passenger motor vehicle transporting a child six years of age or more, but less than 16 years of age, in the front seat of a passenger motor vehicle shall be responsible for securing such child in a properly adjusted and fastened seat safety belt. For the purposes of this section, use of seat safety belts shall include the use of shoulder harnesses where such harness is a standard part of the equipment of the passenger motor vehicle.

(b) All school buses, as defined in Section 1-182 of the Illinois Vehicle Code, codified as 625 ILCS 5/1-182, as amended, that meet the minimum Federal Motor Vehicle Safety Standards 222 for the purposes of transporting children 18 and under shall be equipped with individual set of seat safety belts.... No school bus shall be operated unless all passengers safety belts are fastened.

(c) The provisions of this section shall not apply to:

1) A driver or passenger frequently stopping and leaving the vehicle or delivering property from the vehicle, if the speed of the vehicle between stops does not exceed 15 miles per hour;

2) A driver or passenger possessing a written statement from a physician that he or she is unable for medical or physical reasons to wear a seat safety belt;

3) A driver or passenger possessing a certificate or license endorsement issued by the Motor Vehicle Division of the state or a similar agency in another state or county indicating that the driver or passenger is unable for medical, physical or other valid reasons to wear a seat safety belt;

4) A driver operating a motor vehicle in reverse;

5) A passenger motor vehicle manufactured before January 1, 1965;

6) A motorcycle, motortricycle or moped;

7) Any passenger motor vehicle which is not required to be equipped with seat safety belts under state or federal law, except school buses;

8) A passenger motor vehicle operated by apostal carrier of the United States Postal Service while such carrier is performing his or her duties as a postal carrier; or

9) A school bus transporting students who reside and attend schools situated outside of the city.

(d) Any person who shall violate the provisions of this section shall be fined $25.00

Section 9-76-220 Obstruction of driver's vision; tinted and nonreflective windows

(a) No person shall operate a motor vehicle on any roadway with any sign, poster, window application, reflective material, nonreflective material or tinted film on the front windshield, sidewings or sidewindows immediately adjacent to either side of the operator. A nonrelective tint screen may be used along the uppermost portion of the front windshield if the material does not extent more than six inches down from the top of the windshield.

(b) It is unlawful to park or stand a vehicle on any portion of the public way if the vehicle is equipped with nonreflective, smoked or tinted glass or nonreflective film on the front windshield, sidewings or side windows immediately adjacent to either side of the driver's seat.

(c) It is a defense to a charged violation of subsections (a) or (b) of this section that the motor vehicle complies with the use, medical prescription and documentation provisions of paragraph (g) of Section 12-503 of the Illinois Vehicle Code.

Section 9-80-080 Parking for certain purposes prohibited

(a) It shall be unlawful to park any vehicle upon any roadway for the sole purpose of displaying the vehicle for sale. The vehicle shall be subject to vehicle impoundment...Any person who violates this subsection shall be fined $100.00. Each day the vehicle remains in violation of this subsection shall constitute a separate and distinct offense for which a separate penalty shall be imposed.

(b) No person shall park a vehicle upon any roadway or in any alley to grease or repair the vehicle except for repairs necessitated by an emergency.

(c) No person shall park a vehicle upon any roadway to sell merchandise from such vehicle except in duly established market or pursuant to permit.

This provision regarding putting a for sale sign in your car is subject to interpretation. If you are an individual selling your car and you live in Chicago you are not parked for the "sole purpose" of displaying your vehicle for sale. This provision was designed to prevent car dealers located outside Chicago from putting their vehicles on display in the city. Officers tend to write these tickets anyway.

Section 9-102-20   Red light violation

(a) The registered owner of record of a vehicle is liable for a violation of this section and a fine of $90.00 when the vehicle is used in violation of Section 9-8-020(c) of Section (9 -16-030(c) and that violation is recorded by a traffic control signal monitoring device. A photographic recording of a violation obtained by a traffic control signal monitoring device shall be prima facie evidence of a violation of this chapter.

(b) The provisions of this section do not apply to any authorized emergency vehicle or any vehicle lawfully participating in a funeral procession.

(c) Nothing in this section shall be construed to limit the liability of an operator of a vehicle for any violation.

Grounds for adjudication by mail or administrative hearing for red lights violations.

A person charged with a red-light violation recorded by a traffic control signal monitoring device may contest the charge through an adjudication by mail or administrative hearing limited to one or more of the following grounds with appropriate evidence to support.

1. That the operator of the vehicle was issued a uniform traffic citation for a moving violation;

2. That the violation occurred at any time the vehicle or plates were reported stolen;

3. That the vehicle was leased and the owner submitted the name and address of the lessee;

4. That the vehicle was an authorized emergency vehicle or was in a funeral procession;

5. That the facts alleged in the violation notice are inconsistent or do not support a finding of liability;

6. That the respondent was not the registered owner or lessee of the vehicle at the time of the violation.

- Unless one of the above defenses applies, these are tough tickets to beat. The city has pictures and video of the violation.

CHAPTER FOUR

THE TICKET: PRIMA FACIE CASE

All right, now you've gotten a ticket for a parking and/or compliance violation. You need to examine the ticket closely, because what is written on it (or is omitted) may provide you with a defense. But first, you should know that this type of ticket is what's called a "prima facie" case. What does prima facie mean? In legal terms, prima facie is a Latin phrase that means "at first look," or "on its face." So a prima facie parking violation is one that looks like a parking violation and will be treated as a parking violation unless someone can show evidence to the contrary. The law, as written, is detailed below.

9-100-030 Prima facie responsibility for violation and penalty – Parking violation issuance and removal.

(a) Whenever any vehicle exhibits a compliance violation or is parked in violation of any provision of the traffic code prohibiting or restricting vehicular parking or standing, any person in whose name the vehicle is registered with the Secretary of State of Illinois or such other state's registry of motor vehicles shall be prima facie responsible for the violation and subject to the penalty therefore. The city and the ticketing agent shall accurately record the state registration number of the ticketed vehicle. The prima facie case shall not be established when:

(1) the ticketing agent has failed to specify the proper state registration number of the cited vehicle on the notice;

(2) the city has failed to accurately record the specified state registration number; or

(3) for the purposes of Section 9-64-125, the registered owner was not a resident of the City of Chicago on the day the violation was issued.

(b) Whenever any vehicle exhibits a compliance violation during operation or is parked in violation of any provision of the traffic code prohibiting or restricting vehicular parking or standing or regulating the condition of a parked or standing vehicle, any police officer, traffic control aide, other designated member of the police department, parking enforcement aide or other person designated by the city traffic compliance administrator observing such violation may issue a parking or compliance violation notice, as provided for in Section 9-100-040 and serve the notice on the owner of the vehicle by handing it to the operator of the vehicle, if he is present, or by affixing it to the vehicle in a conspicuous place. The issuer of the notice shall specify on the notice his identification number, the particular parking or compliance ordinance allegedly violated, the make and state registration number of the cited vehicle, and the place, date, time and nature of the alleged violation and shall certify the correctness of the specified information by signing his name as provided.

(c) The city traffic compliance administrator shall withdraw a violation notice when said notice fails to establish a prima facie case as described in this section; provided, however, that a violation notice shall not be withdrawn if the administrator reasonably determines that (1) a state registration number was properly recorded by the city and its ticketing agent, and (2) any discrepancy between the vehicle make or model and the vehicle registration number as set forth in the violation notice is the result of the illegal exchange of registration plates.

(d) It shall be unlawful for any person, other than the owner of the vehicle or his designee, to remove from a vehicle a parking or compliance violation notice affixed pursuant to this chapter.

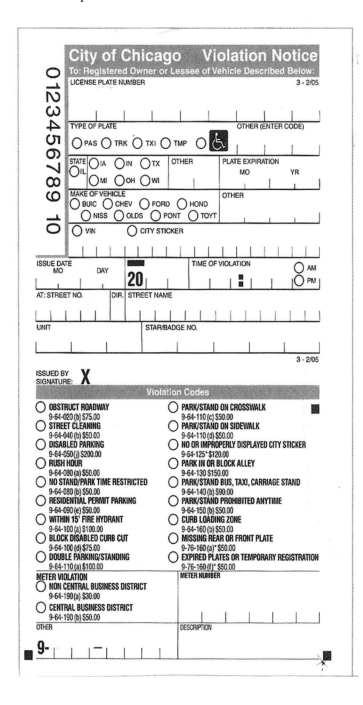

EXPLAINING THE PRIMA FACIE CASE

This section – 9-100-030 – is probably the most important and at the same time most outrageous section of the entire parking code. What does this provision mean? Paragraph (a) informs you that the registered owner of the plates is the one who is responsible for all parking violations, not the driver. Section (b) tells you that a police officer or parking enforcement aide (PEA) needs to either hand you a ticket or affix a ticket to your vehicle. The only problem with first part of section (b) is that, for purposes of contesting your ticket, the DOAH does not require actual "delivery" or the placement of the ticket on your car. The powers that be at the administrative hearing feel that notice by mail is good enough. In other words, the citizen has no way of proving that they didn't receive delivery of the ticket on the vehicle.

Most importantly, paragraph (b) of this section also describes all the necessary elements for a parking violation. These are the elements that hearing officers have used to make the city's prima facie case for years.

1. Proper state registration number of the cited vehicle on the notice;

2. Make of the cited vehicle;

3. Particular parking or compliance ordinance allegedly violated;

4. Place where the alleged violation occurred;

5. Date when the alleged violation occurred;

6. Time when the alleged violation occurred; and

7. Signature of the authorized officer certifying the correctness of the specified information.

If you look at a parking ticket, all of these elements are found on the face of a ticket. These are necessary requirements in order for a ticket to be properly written. In my experience, approximately five percent (1 in 20) or more of all contested tickets were not properly written on their face. One or more of these requirements is incorrect or missing. Should you receive an improperly written ticket, and you contest it, you are home free. If you contest an improperly written ticket on its face, then a hearing officer should dismiss it.

The problem arises when citizens fail to contest their parking tickets. Section (c) of this provision gives Chicago a multimillion dollar free pass. If you read the provision closely, the city is only required to withdraw a violation if the officer fails to list the state registration number on the ticket and/or the plate number doesn't match the make of the vehicle. In other words, even if there is no specific violation, location, date, time or signature, the registered owner of the plate will be drawn into the parking enforcement system. The city will simply begin to send notices. If you are the registered owner of the plate and you don't contest, the ticket will default through the system. If you don't pay or contest within the proper time frame, then the fee for the improperly written ticket will double. Yes! You will actually have to pay double for an improperly written ticket.

The City pulls a nifty trick here. As reasons for withdrawing bad tickets, they limit the prima facie case to inaccuracies in your plate number and/or make of car. In essence, paragraph (c) switches the burden of dealing with improperly written tickets from the city to the citizen. Wouldn't you think that, if an authorized agent of the city writes a bad ticket (one that has other errors), the city should be responsible for withdrawing that ticket prior to sending collection notices and accepting money from you? Does anyone else view this as outrageous?

You're probably asking yourself why the city wouldn't withdraw any violation that fails to establish all of the elements of a properly written ticket. The answer is disturbing but shouldn't surprise you. This would require the DOAH or Department of Revenue to hire staff to review all 2.8 million parking tickets that they issue every year. Not only that, they would be required to withdraw any questionable tickets prior to sending out notices. The city has no interest in paying anyone to spoil and throw out thousands of tickets and millions of dollars. Reviewing every single ticket for these seven elements would be an expensive and time-consuming proposition. Someone apparently had an idea: Why not transfer the legal burden for bad tickets to our citizens? Let's suck our citizens into our administrative adjudication system and force them to play by our rules. That is exactly what they do in paragraph (c). And it works. The city makes millions of dollars every year on improperly written tickets because citizens seem to be more than willing to pay them.

To give you some idea of the enormous impact and amounts of money involved let's do a calculation. Suppose the citizens of Chicago contested the 2.5 million tickets per year that they just pay and only five percent of these tickets fail the prima facie case. That would equal approximately 125,000 tickets per year that should have been dismissed on their face. Multiply 125,000 tickets by $50.00 per ticket, and you get $6.25 million per year. The program has been in effect since September of 1990. Those 17 years at $6.25 million per year equals 106 million dollars.

Statistical sampling of the paid and defaulted parking tickets between 1990 and 2007 would show that this five percent estimate of bad tickets is conservative. I challenge the city to prove me wrong. They won't do this for two reasons. First, they would have to define what the prima facie case actually is under the law and not use their own definition. Second, the city would have to consider returning tens of millions of dollars wrongfully taken from the citizens of Chicago over the last 17 years. Discussion below regarding Problems with "Good" Tickets.

Carefully review your ticket to make sure that each of the seven elements required is properly filled out on the face of the violation. If there is any question regarding the prima facie case, you must contest it.

LESSON: MAKE SURE THAT YOUR TICKET ESTABLISHES THE SEVEN ELEMENTS OF THE PRIMA FACIE CASE. THE ONLY WAY ANYONE WILL REVIEW THE PRIMA FACIE CASE IS IF YOU CONTEST YOUR TICKET.

PROBLEMS WITH "GOOD" TICKETS

What is a good ticket on its face? The prima facie case is not a fixed or simple idea. It is a nuanced concept that can be interpreted by the city and ALOs in many ways. In seventeen years, no Illinois appellate court has ever determined definitively what the prima facie case is. The city of Chicago through the DOAH interprets the prima facie case in any way it deems fit to suit its purposes. Let me give you some examples of how the city's definition of the prima facie case can be interpreted. (The numbers in parenthesis refer to one of the seven elements of a prima facie case listed at the beginning of this chapter.)

Contested tickets issued by parking enforcement aides (PEAs). Do these tickets violate the officer's verification and signature requirement? (#7 above) The parking enforcement aides, in their green jackets, write tickets on their computers. They print out a ticket and place this computer-generated ticket on your vehicle. The prima facie case requires that each ticket be signed by the officer who wrote the ticket so as to verify that the information on the ticket is true and correct. When PEA tickets are contested, all the hearing officer will ever actually see is a signed affidavit showing that the PEA signed off on a range of tickets, not on any individual ticket. Let us say the PEA wrote 75 tickets during her shift. The hearing officer only sees a signed affidavit by the PEA showing the correctness of the ticket range (supposedly all the tickets) and not a verification of any individual ticket. I always thought that this was a big problem with reviewing PEA tickets and wasn't enough to establish the prima facie case. The DOAH thinks that this procedure is adequate to establish the prima facie case. This issue needs to be litigated to the appellate court in order to determine if the prima facie case is established in this circumstance.

Tickets issued at airports. (#4 above) The officer writes O'Hare or Midway as the location of the violation. Is this a specific enough location to establish the prima facie case? O'Hare is the size of many midsized cities. Without a more specific location, for example, a terminal number and an entrance number, I argue there is no prima facie case.

Check-off boxes on tickets for certain violations with multiple offenses (#3 above). Here's the problem: 9-64-130 is an alley-parking violation. When the officer checks off the box on the ticket, is he charging the owner with 130(a) "parking in an alley" or 130(b) "blocking an alley"? The prima facie case requires that the ticket be written indicating the *specific* violation of the ordinance. These are two separate offences that exist within the same ordinance. The citizen has no idea with which violation he is being charged or what defense to raise. In this circumstance, has the prima facie case been established? The same argument holds for other check-off boxes that include multiple violations.

I raise these issues in order to point out that the prima facie case is subject to interpretation by the city and hearing officers. All of these issues need to be litigated at the appellate court level to establish law. Until then, the city through the DOAH, interprets and controls the law and takes your money.

CHAPTER FIVE

DEFENSES AND EXEMPTIONS

DEFENSES

A person charged with a parking or compliance violation may contest the charge through adjudication by mail or at an administrative hearing, limited to one or more of the grounds listed below. You must have appropriate evidence to support your claim.

1. The respondent was not the owner or lessee of the cited vehicle at the time of the violation. (Send in a copy of the state registration for the license plate.)

2. The cited vehicle or its state registration plates had been stolen at the time of the violation. (Send the police report of the theft.)

3. The relevant signs prohibiting or restricting parking were missing or obscured. (Provide details and pictures of the signage on the block.)

4. The relevant parking meter was inoperable or malfunctioned through no fault of the respondent. (Provide the meter number and specific details of the way in which the meter malfunctioned. Report the meter broken on day of ticket.)

5. The facts alleged in the parking or compliance violation notice are inconsistent or do not support a finding that the specified regulation was violated. (This is a catch-all category. Provide the appropriate evidence.)

6. The illegal condition described in the compliance violation notice did not exist at the time the notice was issued. (Another catch-all category. Again, provide appropriate evidence for your claim.)

7. The compliance violation was corrected prior to adjudication of the charge. However, in the words of the ordinance "this defense shall not be applicable to compliance violations involving display of the city wheel tax emblem [city sticker] under Section 9-64-125; [or] to compliance violations involving motor vehicle exhaust systems under subsection (a) of Section (2) of Section 9-76-160; [or] to compliance violations involving display of temporary registration or temporary permits under subsection (f) of Section 9-76-160; or

to compliance violations relating to glass coverings or coating under Section 9-76-220." (With the exception of the prohibitions listed, provide evidence that the compliance violation was corrected before your hearing or mail adjudication.)

FOR A HEARING OFFICER TO DISMISS A TICKET, YOU MUST RAISE ONE OF THE ABOVE DEFENSES. THESE ARE THE DEFENSES THAT APPLY TO EVERY TICKET.

EXEMPTIONS

Although the previously listed defenses are the only ones permitted, in some instances you may be exempt from paying a fine due to extenuating circumstances. The code (as written) below describes those circumstances.

Section 9-64-10 Applicability-Exemptions

(a) The provisions of the traffic code prohibiting the standing or parking of vehicles shall apply at all times or at those times therein specified or as indicated on official signs, where required, except when it is necessary to stop a vehicle to avoid conflict with other traffic or in compliance with the directions of a police officer, traffic control aide or official traffic-control device.

IF YOU ACTED TO AVOID AN ACCIDENT AND/OR AT THE DIRECTION OF A POLICE OFFICER OR TRAFFIC CONTROL AIDE, YOU SHOULD BE EXEMPT.

(b) The provisions of any ordinance imposing a time limit on parking shall not relieve any person from the duty to observe other and more restrictive provisions prohibiting or limiting the standing or parking of vehicles in specified places or at specified times.

THIS PROVISION DESCRIBES A PARKING RULE AND IS NOT REALLY AN EXEMPTION. IF THERE IS MORE THAN ONE RESTRICTION COVERING YOUR SPOT, YOU ARE SUBJECT TO THE PROVISIONS OF ALL SIGNAGE COVERING THE SPOT INCLUDING THE MOST RESTRICTIVE.

(c) Notwithstanding any other provisions of the traffic code, any motor vehicle bearing handicapped or disabled veterans' state registration plates or a handicapped parking decal or device…from Illinois or any other jurisdiction designating the vehicle is operated by or for a handicapped person is hereby exempt from the payment of parking meter fees and exempt from any ordinance or regulation which imposes a time limitation for parking…This exemption shall not be construed to authorize the parking of any vehicle during hours when parking is otherwise prohibited or where the vehicle constitutes a traffic hazard and must be moved at the instruction and request of a law enforcement officer. The exemption granted under this subsection shall apply only when the motor vehicle is operated by or under the personal direction of the person for whom the handicapped or disabled veteran registration plates or handicapped parking decal or device was issued.

IF YOU ARE THE REGISTERED OWNER AND HANDICAPPED AND YOU EXHIBITED A HANDICAPPED PLACARD OR PLATES, YOU ARE EXEMPT FROM PAYING METERS OR FINES FOR ANY VIOLATION FOR TIME RESTRICTION. YOU MUST HAVE BEEN PRESENT AT THE TIME.

Lessor of vehicle not liable for violations—When

(a) In accordance with Section 11-1306 of the Illinois Vehicle Code, no person who is the lessor of a vehicle pursuant to a written lease agreement shall be liable for a violation of any standing or parking regulation of this chapter involving such vehicle during the period of the lease if upon receipt of a notice of violation sent with 120 days of the violation he shall, within 60 days thereafter, provide to the city traffic compliance administrator the name and address of the lessee.

(b) Upon receipt of a lessor's notification of the name and address of his lessee, provided pursuant to Sections 11-1305 and 11-1306 of the Illinois Vehicle Code, the city traffic compliance administrator shall cause a notice of violation to be sent to the lessee as provided for in Section 9-100-050(d)

WITH RENTAL VEHICLES, THE RENTER (LESSEE), NOT THE RENTAL COMPANY (LESSOR), IS RESPONSIBLE FOR ANY PARKING TICKETS. DEPENDING ON WHETHER YOU ARE THE LESSOR OR THE LESSEE, YOU MAY OR MAY NOT BE EXEMPT.

NOTE: *Lending* your car to someone else who gets a ticket while using your vehicle is not the same thing. As the registered owner, you are responsible for any tickets received. (Although the person to whom you lent the car may generously give you the money, you are still responsible for sending in the fine or contesting the ticket.)

Section 9-100-150 Owner of vehicle not liable for violations when in custody of valet.

(a) In accordance with Section 4-232-080(b) of this Code, no person who is the owner of a vehicle shall be liable for a violation of any parking or compliance regulation of this chapter involving such vehicle during the period that such vehicle was in the custody of a valet parking service, if upon receipt of a notice of violation sent within 120 days of the violation he shall, within 60 days thereafter, provide to the city traffic compliance administrator the valet parking receipt required by Section 4-232-080(d) of this Code or a clearly legible copy thereof.

(b) Upon receipt of the valet parking receipt or copy and upon being satisfied that it is genuine and not altered and that the violation took place while the vehicle was in the custody of the valet parking service as shown by the times indicated on the receipt, the city traffic compliance administrator shall cause a notice of violation to be sent to the valet parking service as provided for in Section 9-100-050(d).

A VALET SERVICE IS RESPONSIBLE FOR ALL TICKETS DURING THE TIME OF SERVICE. ALWAYS KEEP YOUR VALET RECEIPTS BECAUSE THE VIOLATION NOTICE

MAY BE YOUR FIRST INDICATION THAT YOU HAVE RECEIVED A TICKET. THIS COULD BE 14 DAYS AFTER THE VIOLATION.

CHAPTER SIX

CONTESTING YOUR TICKET

According to the city, motorists have the right to timely challenge any tickets believed to be issued in error. According to the law, motorists have the right to timely challenge *any* ticket issued. Motorists also have the right to an impartial and independent review by an Administrative Law Officer and to appeal liable decisions to the Circuit Court of Cook County.

You've studied the defenses and exemptions, and you've determined that you have a good case. Now what? How do you contest your ticket? You can either do it by mail or you can request an in-person hearing, but whichever method you choose, you must do it in a timely way or you'll lose your right to contest.

PROCEDURE TO CONTEST: REQUEST A HEARING

Request a hearing before your right to a hearing expires. If you fail to respond to a ticket, you will receive a mailed notice of violation. If you do not respond to the notice of violation within 14 days from the date it was issued, a determination of liability will automatically be entered against you. After 14 days from the date on your violation notice, you can no longer contest by mail. After your determination notice, you still have 21 days to contest in person by filing a petition to set aside the determination and, if granted, receive an immediate hearing. After 21 days, a final determination will be entered against you, and an amount equal to the original fine will also be assessed. When the ticket has reached final determination, the fine will have doubled, and you will have lost your right to contest it.

IN-PERSON VERSUS MAIL-IN HEARINGS

The debate regarding whether to contest in person or by mail has been going on since the inception of the program in 1990. This controversy has become part of urban parking legend in Chicago. There are no publicly available statistics that would indicate an advantage or disadvantage of using either method. What can be said is that there are distinct advantages and disadvantages to each method, depending on your personality, time available and your personal preference.

Would you rather present your defense face to face or are you more persuasive writing a cogent letter? Do you enjoy public speaking or do you communicate best by writing?

Would you rather seek redress in public or remain anonymous? Would you like to receive your decision immediately after your hearing or can you wait for weeks to get your response by mail? These are some of the many considerations in determining whether to contest in person or by mail. I happen to be a person who likes to contest by mail. After reading this chapter you can decide for yourself which you prefer.

Whether you contest by mail or in person, beating your parking ticket is all about preparation for your hearing. How to be best prepared for your hearing: first, know what violation you're charged with. Second, state which defense or defenses you're arguing. Third, provide copies of all supporting and relevant documents and evidence.

NOTE: In 2007, of the 117,746 parking tickets contested by mail 62% were dismissed and of the 142,594 parking tickets contested in person 56% were dismissed.

CONTESTING BY MAIL

To contest by mail, fill in the contest-by-mail box on the ticket envelope and include a signed statement explaining your defense. If you do not respond to the original ticket you will receive a mailed violation notice. You still have 14 days from the date of this violation notice to contest by mail. The name of the registered owner appearing on the vehicle's license plate registration must sign the statement. (If this is not you, the ticket is the responsibility of the owner.) Enclose any other evidence to support your claim including, but not limited to, police reports, registration documents, receipts and pictures. Enclose copies, as evidence will not be returned. Mail your challenge in the envelope provided or write to the mailing address below:

> Chicago Department of Revenue
> P.O. Box 88298
> Chicago IL 60680-1298

Contesting by mail is much easier and is more impersonal. You can write a letter and present whatever documentary evidence you have and then wait for your decision in the mail. With an envelope, paper and a 42 cent stamp you can raise a valid defense from the comfort of your home. The ALO will never see you or form an opinion about you other than what you write in your letter. You can present any relevant evidence that you would be able to present in an in-person hearing.

When you write a letter, the ALO can't question you. All the ALO can use to make a decision is the letter and evidence presented. Will the ALO give you the benefit of the doubt regarding questions he or she may have? I always did. Some argue that it is much easier for an ALO to find liability by pressing a button on his computer when you are not present. Although there is no statistical evidence that would establish this, I always found it easier. That doesn't mean that I found more people liable who contested by mail versus those who appeared in person. All it means is that when I did find someone liable, it was easier to press a button than to have to tell them. Weighing the economic implications of a $50.00 ticket, running to a hearing facility seems like a huge waste of time. In our busy lives, taking a little time to prepare a proper letter with the potential reward of a "not-liable" decision seems to make sense.

What are the ALOs doing and thinking when they decide your contest by mail? Although a hearing officer can decide a mail-in case from his or her computer in any hearing room, he or she is most likely sitting in a large room on the second floor at the central hearing facility referred to as the "mail-in room." The mail-in room is set up with two long rows of computers on either side. The ALOs sit at their computers for two three-and-a-half hour sessions every day from 9:00 a.m. until 12:30 p.m. and from 1:30 p.m. until 5:00 p.m. pulling mail in cases from a work queue of hundreds of cases. Once they pull up a case, they review images of the entire case ticket and letter, then make decisions. The entire process takes from 5 to 10 minutes per case. As you can imagine, this is an extremely tedious and boring procedure. Most ALOs will process between 20 and 30 tickets per session.

When writing your defense letter, your objective is to convince the hearing officer to dismiss your ticket. All you can really do is provide the hearing officer with everything they need to do this. The letter should make the hearing officer's job as simple as possible. You can do this by writing and signing a short cogent letter citing your defense and including copies of supporting evidence. Make sure that your spelling and grammar are correct. A well-written and concise letter is more credible than one that rambles on or gives irrelevant information. (See the end of the chapter for some sample letters.)

IMAGING PROBLEMS WITH MAILED-IN MATERIALS

Sometimes when a hearing officer reviews a contest by mail there are imaging or other computer problems. Perhaps the ticket itself or the letter or pictures that the citizen provided were not properly imaged, or the PEA verification signature is missing from a ticket issued by a parking enforcement aide. When this occurs, the ALO is required by the DOAH's policy to fill out a "Problem Log" describing what is wrong with the case, turn it over to the city and move on to the next mail-in hearing. In effect, the ALOs are continuing the case on behalf of the city, until the city is ready to proceed. (You are not notified about these problems, and you don't have to do anything, but such problems will delay adjudication.)

The City claims that ALOs are independent. ALOs are not the city's attorneys, yet they continue a ticket without a motion by the city, if there is an imaging problem and the city's case is lacking. When I was a hearing officer, my view was that since it was the city's responsibility to properly process and image the ticket, letter and evidence, and a case was placed by the city in the mail-in work queue, when a hearing officer pulled up that case, the city should have been ready for the hearing at that time. Why should the city get another bite at the apple or another chance to present its case? The citizen doesn't get this opportunity. If the city isn't prepared for the hearing, then the ticket should be dismissed. I always found that this problem-log procedure was entirely inappropriate for a supposedly independent hearing officer.

NOTE: Under the parking law each ticket should be treated individually, however, when conducting hearings, the ALO has access to a computer system that allows them to obtain your entire ticket history and secretary of state records.

TIME VALUE OF MONEY AND COST TO CONTEST BY MAIL

Is it worth 42 cents for the stamp to have your ticket reviewed by mail? If you can put off paying your ticket for several weeks, the interest from holding your money will pay for the stamp.

- $50.00 parking ticket: $50.00 in an interest-bearing saving account at 3% interest = $1.50 annually. Divide by 52 weeks = 2.88 cents per week Break even = 15 weeks

- $100.00 parking ticket: $100.00 in a saving account at 3% interest = $3.00 annually. Divide by 52 weeks = 5.77 cents per week. Break even = 7 weeks.

You may find this analysis ridiculous but don't think for one second that the city of Chicago's Department of Revenue doesn't look at your payments in exactly the same way. As far as the city is concerned, it's all about when they get paid. It's time that we as citizens think strategically.

CONTESTING IN PERSON

To contest in person, fill in the "request for in-person hearing" box on the ticket envelope to make your request by mail. To make your request by phone, call 312-744-PARK. You can also drop off your request at any parking hearing facility. You will receive notification by mail informing you of which week you are to show up for your in-person hearing. You can come to a hearing facility any day during that week from Monday through Friday between 8 a.m. and 4 p.m. Bring to the hearing any evidence you wish to have considered including, but not limited to, police reports, registration documents, receipts and pictures, affidavits and witnesses.

Whether your experience at the hearing facility will be reasonably pleasant or an ordeal is partly up to you. When you arrive at the facility, you will have to wait in line for the DOAH clerk to check you in. This individual can be your best friend or your worst enemy. These people take more verbal abuse than any other city employees. I mean any city employee in any department. They are my personal heroes. Be polite and respectful to them. They are the individuals who can answer your questions and help you navigate the system. They also determine to which hearing room you will be assigned.

PROCEDURE IN THE HEARING ROOM:

Once you are sent into a hearing room, enter quietly and take a seat. If the hearing room is crowded, you may have to wait for a while. The hearing rooms operate as first come first served. Be patient. Wait for your turn to be called up to the podium. Listen and learn from your ALO and the other cases.

The nature of our administrative hearings is not as complex as judicial court proceedings. The strict rules of evidence and procedure are not applicable, and plain language is used as opposed to legal jargon. Although some people hire attorneys to represent them, most choose to represent themselves. The hearing is open to the public. The hearings follow a basic structure to give the appearance of fairness and due process of law. The hearing officer will begin by giving his or her opening remarks, which outline the hearing process. All testimony is under oath and recorded.

Since the city initiated the case, it has to present its evidence before you have an opportunity to say a word or present a defense. The city is required to establish the prima facie case. That simply means that it must set forth the necessary allegations that a code violation has occurred. With parking tickets, the sworn notice of violation is all that is required. The police officer or parking enforcement aide is not required to be present at the hearing. The hearing officer reviews the city's case to see if it has alleged all the necessary elements required by law. If the city hasn't properly alleged its case, the case will be dismissed.

If the city has properly alleged a case, the hearing will proceed to the next phase, and you will have the opportunity to present your defense. YOU'RE ON! This is your opportunity to contest the allegations and/or present your side of the story. Be polite yet confident.

Raise your specific defense and introduce proof such as testimony, a sworn affidavit, testimony of witnesses or other evidence such as photographs, receipts, police reports or other documents.

After both sides have had an opportunity to present their cases, the hearing officer will render a decision and written order. The city's burden of proof in these matters is by a preponderance of the evidence, which means that taking everything into consideration, the hearing officer must believe that it is more likely than not that a code violation has occurred. If the hearing officer doesn't believe the city has a preponderance of evidence, you will be found not liable. You've won your case. Collect your decision; thank the hearing officer and leave. If you are found liable, remain calm. There is absolutely no reason to pitch a tantrum at this point.

Either side may appeal the hearing officer's decision to the Circuit Court of Cook County (Richard J. Daley Center, 50 W Washington, 6th Floor) within 35 days by filing a civil lawsuit for administrative review and by paying the applicable state filing fee. (A pauper's petition allows you to appeal for free.) The city of Chicago has never appealed a hearing officer decision in seventeen years.

An in-person hearing allows you to present your case to an ALO face to face. Some people believe that ALOs will be more sympathetic if you're in front of them. Some people argue that an ALO will be less likely to tell you to your face that you are responsible for your ticket. There is no publicly available statistical evidence to show that this is true. Most seasoned hearing officers have no problem telling you that you're responsible for paying your ticket. The real problem with an in-person hearing is that the ALO can form an opinion about you based on your appearance or demeanor. He or she can ask you difficult questions, listen to your voice, look into your eyes and make a judgment as to whether or not you're telling the truth. Another issue regarding contesting in person is that the registered owner (you) or your attorney or authorized agent has to show up at a hearing facility during hearing hours, which may also be work or business hours for you. You can waste an incredible amount of time in line and in a hearing room waiting for your opportunity to be heard. If you are going to have an in-person hearing, show up by 8 a.m. so that you can be first in line.

WHAT IF YOU ARE FOUND LIABLE

Regardless of the type of hearing you choose, you may be found liable. If you are found liable, you have three choices:

1. Pay within 7 days to avoid having the fine double.

2. Appeal the decision to the Circuit Court within 35 days. If you lose, the fine will have already doubled, and you will have court costs (unless you obtain a pauper's petition at the Circuit Court.)

3. This is a long shot: write a letter to the Director of the Department of Administrative Hearings and request an administrative release. Good luck! An administrative release is given at the discretion of the director, and one is usually given only for media cases that would otherwise make the DOAH or the Department of Revenue look bad.

MOTION TO SET ASIDE DEFAULT DETERMINATION

Suppose, despite all this good advice, you just ignored your ticket and let time run out until the city made a determination by default. Is there anything you can do now? Yes, you can file a motion to set aside the default determination.

If you want to file a motion to set aside the notice of determination, then you will have to appear in person at a hearing facility during the hours previously specified. Pursuant to section 2-14-108 of the Municipal Code of Chicago, a person may file a written motion to set aside a default order. The DOAH clerk will provide you with a motion form which you can fill out prior to entering a hearing room. In general, the motion must:

1. Be filed within 21 days after the issuance of the default order (the date that the default order was deposited in the U.S. mail);

2. Present a good-cause reason for your prior failure to appear for the hearing. In essence you have to explain why you didn't respond to your ticket prior to this date. At this time, you can give any excuses or reasons why you haven't contested yet.

A hearing officer has the discretion to grant or deny the motion to set aside. Most ALOs are reasonable and will grant the motion giving you a hearing on the merits of the ticket. However, some hearing officers will deny your motion for one reason or another, claiming your reason wasn't good-cause. You must also be prepared to proceed with an immediate hearing if the motion is granted. So bring all your evidence and any witnesses. If you have multiple tickets and motions, show up at the hearing facility early. Nothing is more annoying to an ALO than having to process multiple motions and hearings at the end of the day.

PREPARING FOR THE HEARING

If you are going to appear before a hearing officer, whether you win or lose your ticket will depend on your preparation for the hearing.

You need to structure your defense in three parts:

1) What violation am I charged with?
2) What defense applies?
3) What proof will I need to establish or prove my defense?

The evidence that you present must be relevant to your defense. Your evidence could include one or all of the items below:

- Your testimony

- Witness testimony

- Copies of affidavits and/or notarized statements

- Copies of police reports that you filed when the incident(s) occurred. It is important to file promptly. Such reports might include:

  - stolen vehicles,

  - stolen plates,

  - stolen plate registration stickers,

  - and stolen city stickers and permits.

  NOTE: Chicago police department will also issue a Miscellaneous Incident Report in certain circumstances. This report reflects situations that do not rise to a theft. (eg. Your front plate gets knocked off by vandals and you receive a ticket on that day.)

  - Copies of state registration documents. (The city mails all notices to the address on your license plate registration, so it's important to update your address with the Illinois Secretary of State within 10 days of moving.)

  - Copies of city sticker/permits/handicapped placards

  - Copies of receipts

  - Pictures. Keep a camera in your car to document the scene of a ticket. Pictures are a huge help in your defense. Take pictures of the entire area and one of the street signs to make sure that you identify the location. Document the time and date on the photo. Pictures that only show a portion of the block are a big turnoff for hearing officers.

MODEL LETTERS

Letter 1 for Defense #4:

Dear Hearing Officer:

I have been charged with ticket # _____ violating 9-64-190(a) non business district meter. I am raising the defense that the meter malfunctioned through no fault of my own. In support of this defense I parked at meter #23657 on January 8, 2007 at 3:10 pm. I fed the meter one quarter for 30 minutes' time. The meter took my money but did not register the quarter. I tried to put another quarter in the meter, and the same thing happened. I came back to the car within 30 minutes at 3:35 p.m., and I had received a ticket. Your records should reflect that I called and reported the meter broken.

Thank you for your time and consideration.

Sincerely,

John Doe (Signature of registered owner)

Letter 2 for Defense #5:

Dear Hearing Officer:

I have been charged with ticket # _____ for violating 9-64-200 for parking outside the metered space. I am raising the defense that the facts alleged in the ticket were inconsistent and failed to establish that a violation occurred. In support of my defense, I present pictures showing where I was parked in a free spot after last metered spot. The law requires pavement markings to identify the meter spots. The pictures show that there are no pavement marking at the location where I parked.

Thank you for your time and consideration.

Sincerely,

John Doe (Signature of registered owner)

Letter 3 for Defense #5

Dear Hearing Officer:

I have been charged with ticket # _____ for violating 9-64-100(a) parking within 15 feet of a fire hydrant. I am respectfully raising the defense that the facts alleged in the ticket are inconsistent. I parked my vehicle at this location at 3:30 p.m. on the date of the ticket. I parked beyond the hydrant with my rear bumper 17 feet from the hydrant. In support of my defense, I've enclosed several pictures taken at the time of the supposed violation. Although my vehicle was parked within the yellow curb markings, I was not in violation of the ordinance. Please note that these pictures indicate with a tape measure that the yellow curb marking extends more than 18 feet from the hydrant.

Thank you for your time and consideration.

Sincerely,

John Doe (Signature of registered owner)

Letter 4 for Defense #5

Dear Hearing Officer:

I received ticket # _____ for violating 9-64-130(a) parking in an alley. I am respectfully raising the defense that the facts alleged in the ticket are inconsistent. At the time and date of the violation 10:30 pm on October, 15, 2007 I was delivering groceries to my aunt, Ms. Sylvia Jones. I was parked in the alley behind her apartment while unloading these groceries. I was inside the apartment when the officer wrote the ticket. I did not stay at my aunts' home any longer than was necessary to deliver these groceries. Enclosed is my receipt from the grocery store showing the time and date of purchase and proof that my aunt lives at the location where I received the ticket.

Thank you for your time and consideration.

Sincerely,

John Doe (Signature of registered owner)

CHAPTER SEVEN

IN THE MIND OF A HEARING OFFICER

According to the city, a hearing officer is a licensed Illinois attorney appointed to preside over the hearing as an independent, fair and impartial judge. A hearing officer does not represent either party.

When contesting a ticket, the administrative law officer (ALO), otherwise known as a hearing officer, is the one person you need to convince to dismiss your ticket. Regarding your parking violations, an ALO is the equivalent of a Supreme Court justice. Although you have a right to appeal his or her decision, for all practical purposes, appealing a $50.00 dollar parking ticket to the Circuit Court of Cook County is not worth your time, money or effort. I've dedicated an entire chapter to the discussion of hearing officers because these are the people you must sway to dismiss your ticket.

Who are these people? How are they selected? How are they trained? What conditions do they work under? How are they compensated? What motivates them to make a decision for or against you? Are they really as fair and impartial as the city presents? We need to address all of these issues in order for you to understand the hearing officer's mentality and motivations. Understanding the hearing officer will increase your odds of convincing him or her to dismiss your ticket.

There are approximately 75-100 hearing officers working for the DOAH at any given time. Some 30 to 40 of them work for the parking enforcement division. Most of these ALOs are part-time, while others are closer to full-time employees, working 40 hours per week. I was a hearing officer for 15 years, and I can tell you from experience that it was often a difficult and sometimes impossible job. The hearing officers are the public face for administrative hearings. They have the often-conflicting responsibility of enforcing an oppressive ordinance while ensuring that citizens feel they have been treated fairly. Essentially, they stand between a rock and a hard place.

I've known many hearing officers over my 15 years with the city. Each hearing officer is a unique individual. A defense that works for one may or may not work with another. Some will treat you with respect while others are rude and obnoxious. Some work with robotic speed while others are agonizingly slow. Some hearing officers are entirely incompetent while others are extremely efficient and intelligent. Some hearing officers take a more liberal view of the ordinance, while others take a narrow and strict interpretation of the parking law. The point here is that every ALO is different, and we must treat them as such.

Whether you contest in person or by mail you cannot forum-shop or choose your hearing officer. It is entirely random as to which ALO hears your ticket. A minority of hearing officers will find you liable no matter what evidence you present. With these ALOs, you have absolutely no chance of beating your ticket. I would rather throw myself into oncoming traffic than have my ticket heard by one of these officers. Thankfully, most ALOs are reasonable professionals trying to do the best job that they can under difficult circumstances. All you can do is make their jobs as easy as possible by giving them as much credible evidence as you can, helping them to rule in your favor.

Hearing officers are political appointees of the Director of the Department of Administrative Hearings. These are plum patronage positions that pay $60.00 per hour. All recent hires are politically connected attorneys or past judges with a minimum of three years of legal experience. Initially, the responsibility to train the parking hearing officers lies with the parking enforcement division chief who happens to be a past prosecutor for the city. The ALOs are trained regarding the parking law, conducting hearings and operating the computer system. The city maintains that all hearing officers receive additional and continual training regardless of their respective legal backgrounds and competence. I found that most of these additional lectures and field training satisfied the letter of the law but were an enormous waste of time. The ALOs actually gain experience and competence by conducting hearings.

The DOAH likes to market itself and its hearing officers as a department that provides due process and fairness to citizens. According to the city's Parking Ticket & Compliance Bill of Rights, motorists have the right to impartial and independent reviews of their tickets by ALOs. The ALOs are depicted as independent decision makers who base their decisions only on their interpretation of the law. The reality of hearing officer life is much different. The ALOs are under constant pressure, and their decisions are heavily monitored and influenced by DOAH policies and procedures. If an ALO wants to work at DOAH, he or she had better play by the rules established by the administration.

To give you some idea of how the DOAH influences and controls its ALOs, all you need to do is consider how they are compensated. An ALO is an independent contractor. Don't let the independent contractor title deceive you. Independent contractor status is a legal and tax term, and it doesn't mean that ALOs are truly independent when deciding your ticket. The ALOs receive an hourly wage with no benefits. They have absolutely no job security and can be taken off the hearing schedule at a DOAH administrator's whim.

An ALO's life involves working long hours. They turn in their time requests by the 10th of the current month and are assigned their days and hours for the following month. In other words, the DOAH decides on a monthly basis how many hours each ALO will receive. Certain full-time hearing officers can make approximately $9,000-$10,000 per month. Even though the hearing officer is supposed to be independent, this compensation structure has a very powerful influence in the mind of every hearing officer at DOAH. If the ALO does something that either his division chief or the director finds objectionable, the division chief/director can either limit the ALO's hours or keep that person off the schedule. This is the most direct method that DOAH has of controlling their hearing officers. It's simple: ALOs who want to work at the DOAH had better make DOAH happy. Who does the ALO work for? Does he work for the benefit of the city or the citizen? You can decide for yourself whether this type of compensation structure influences the hearing officer on a ticket-by-ticket basis.

An ALO's obligation under the law is to conduct a fair hearing. The DOAH has established a hearing form and procedures that create the illusion of a fair hearing. It is the ALOs themselves who determine whether they conduct a fair hearing in substance.

Our entire purpose involves insisting that each hearing officer regardless of outside pressures follows the law. He or she must review the city's ticket to determine if it was properly written and signed. Once the city's prima facie case is established, then the ALO must consider all the evidence presented by the citizen before making a decision on the ticket.

The standard to which an ALO must adhere in making his or her decisions is called a "preponderance of the evidence." It is the cities burden, not the citizens, to establish a preponderance of the evidence in its favor. According to Black's Law Dictionary, a preponderance means: "Evidence which is of greater weight or more convincing than the evidence which is offered in opposition to it; that is evidence which as a whole shows that the fact sought to be proved is more probable than not. The word preponderance denotes a superiority of weight, or outweighing …Yet a judge cannot properly act upon the weight of evidence, in favor of the one having the onus unless it overbears, in some degree, the weight upon the other side."

This is all hearing officers do. With every contested ticket, they ask themselves, "Has the city proven its case by a preponderance of the evidence?" The city's entire case is written on your parking ticket. According to the parking ordinance, if the ticket is properly written on its face it is evidence of the correctness of the facts alleged. The objective of your defense is to refute the city's case. The ALO has the responsibility to determine if your defense has met this objective and if so, to dismiss your ticket.

Remember, the law does not require you to create a preponderance of the evidence in your favor in order to have the ticket dismissed. Under the law this burden is entirely with the city. Determining if the city has established the greater weight of evidence is something of a judgment call. Clearly, the same defense and evidence that negates the cities preponderance in one hearing officer's mind may or may not in another. A large portion of this book is designed to help you present your hearing officer with the best defense possible to rebut the city's case. In other words, if the city presents a properly written ticket and you can present a defense that reduces the cities case to even a 50% - 50% tie in the mind of the hearing officer, the ticket should be dismissed.

NOTE: HELP THE HEARING OFFICER HELP YOU:

When you are concise and provide the hearing officer with everything that he or she needs to make a decision, you are helping the hearing officer. You are helping them in a very real and practical way. The hearing officer has a job to do. During a mail-in session of 3 ½ hours or 210 minutes the ALO should complete 20-30 hearings. With normal breaks of 10 minutes per hour that leaves approximate 7-9 minutes on average per ticket. When you provide a clear defense and relevant evidence not only are you more credible but the ALO doesn't have to waste his or her time deciphering your case. I believe that by simply helping the hearing officer be more efficient you will have already increased your odds of having your ticket dismissed.

CONCLUSION

PARKING BATTLES AND TICKET WARS

Do we live in a civil society? We've all felt the rage and the irrational thoughts that go along with finding parking. One must ask oneself, "Just how crazy am I about finding parking in Chicago?" Have you ever fought over a parking space? Have you been willing to sacrifice life and limb, screaming obscenities at a total stranger for that last legal spot? What about saying to yourself, "I'm going to slash the tires of the person who stole my space?" Or, "I'm a law abiding citizen, but I'm willing to get arrested for that particular spot." Have you ever been in a stand-off where two cars are blocking each other trying to pull into the same spot? Have you ever been approaching an open space on the correct side of the street and someone pulls an illegal U-turn and steals it from you? Otherwise rational people snap when it comes to parking in the city.

There are no real winners in these parking-space battles. One driver will have the satisfaction of getting the space with the associated paranoia that the loser might vandalize her vehicle. The other driver will have to keep wasting gas and his life looking for another spot. Parking has become a zero sum game, a competitive sport similar to musical chairs. There is no parking for second place. These skirmishes focus our attention on our fellow citizens. We become distracted and direct our anger toward another person who is equally as frustrated as we are with finding parking.

Private parking lots have become outrageously expensive, and there are far too many cars without enough legal street parking. With all the parking signs and restrictions on every block, it seems as if the city is intentionally taking away perfectly safe parking areas. The city would like us to believe that if there were no parking restrictions life would be reduced to chaos and our citizens would behave like barbarians. The real battle regarding parking in Chicago is not between its citizens but between its citizens and the city. The real fight is purely economic. This real war has to do with the $160 million per year the city generates from parking tickets.

The primary purpose of this book is to help level the playing field between citizen and city. Up until now all the advantages are with the city. The deck is stacked against you. First, the City Council has established a strict parking ordinance and an enforcement system with teeth. Second, the city has a literal army of police officers and parking enforcement aides to write parking tickets. Third, even if these agents issue you a bad ticket, they don't withdraw it, and you are ensnared by the administrative system. What chance does the individual have against such odds?

The public deserves accurate information regarding the parking law. Knowledge is power. Understanding the law and signage will allow you to avoid unnecessary tickets if you so choose. If you do receive a ticket, exercise your right to contest. The parking war is fought one ticket at a time. As citizens, we must realize that we control the process. We possess the ultimate weapon of mass empowerment, the law of large numbers. CONTEST YOUR TICKETS!

APPENDIX A

HEARING FACILITIES

SOUTH SIDE

2006 E. 95th Street
Payments and Inquires: 8a.m. -5 p.m. (Monday)
8 a.m. - 6:30 p.m. (Tuesday-Friday)
8 a.m. - 3:30 p.m. (Saturday)

Hearing Hours: 8 a.m. - 4 p.m. (Monday-Friday)

NORTH SIDE

2550 W. Addison
Payments and Inquires: 8a.m. - 5 p.m. (Monday)
8 a.m. - 6:30 p.m. (Tuesday-Friday)
8 a.m. - 3:30 p.m. (Saturday)

Hearing Hours: 8 a.m. - 4 p.m. (Monday-Friday)

CENTRAL HEARING FACILITY

400 W. Superior 1st Floor
Payments and Inquires: 8:30a.m. -4:30 p.m. (Monday-Friday)
8:30 a.m. - 3:30 p.m. (Saturday)

Hearing Hours: 9 a.m. - 4 p.m. (Monday-Friday)
Boot hearing also available on Saturdays 9 a.m. -3 p.m.

MAILING ADDRESS:

Payments and Hearing Requests Only
Chicago Department of Revenue
P.O. Box 88298
Chicago IL 60680-1298

TELEPHONE

312-744-7275

EMAIL

Cityofchicago.org/revenue (For payment and status of hearing requests)

TRAFFIC DEFINITIONS AND GENERAL PROVISIONS (9-4)

Adjudication by mail. An administrative process by which a registered owner of a vehicle or his attorney may submit documentary evidence by mail to a hearing officer in order to contest liability for a parking violation.

Administrative hearing. A hearing in person before a hearing officer at which a registered owner of a vehicle or his attorney may contest liability for a parking violation.

Alley. A public way intended to give access to the rear or side of lots or buildings and not intended for the purpose of vehicular through-traffic.

Business street. The length of any street between street intersections on which more than 50 percent of the entire frontage at ground level of the street is in use by retail or wholesale businesses, hotels, banks, office buildings, railway stations, or public buildings other than schools.

Crosswalk. That portion of a roadway ordinarily included within the prolongation or connection of sidewalk lines at intersections or any other portion of a roadway clearly indicated for pedestrian crossing by markings.

Determination of parking violation liability or nonliability. The finding of liability or nonliability for a parking violation reached by a hearing officer after consideration of documentary evidence submitted for adjudication by mail, after an administrative hearing at which the registered owner or his attorney appears to contest liability for a parking violation, or after the registered owner has failed to appear at a requested administrative hearing or failed to respond to a second notice of violation.

Driveway or private road. Every way or place in private ownership and used for vehicular travel by the owner and those having express or implied permission from the owner but not by other persons.

Final determination of parking violation liability. A hearing officer's determination becomes a final determination for purposes of the Administrative Review Law of Illinois upon the exhaustion or failure to exhaust procedures for administrative or judicial review.

Fire lane. Every way or place in private ownership used expressly for vehicular travel by emergency equipment and marked as such by signs or pavement markings.

Parking (to park). The standing of an unoccupied vehicle otherwise than temporarily for the purpose of and while actually engaged in loading or unloading property or passengers.

Parkway. Any portion of a street not considered as roadway, sidewalk, driveway or private road. The area in between the curb and sidewalk.

Second notice of parking violation. The notice, mailed to the address supplied to the Secretary of State by the registered owner of a vehicle, sent after the registered owner has failed to respond within the time allotted by ordinance to a parking violation notice placed on or given to the driver of such vehicle.

Sidewalk. That portion of a public way between the curb, or the lateral lines of the roadway, and the adjacent property lines, intended for the use of pedestrians.

Standing (to stand). The halting of a vehicle, whether occupied or not, otherwise than temporarily for the purpose of and while actually engaged in receiving or discharging passengers provided, that an operator is either in the vehicle or in the immediate vicinity, so as to be capable of immediately moving the vehicle at the direction of a police officer or traffic control aide.

APPENDIX B

Parking and Standing Violations

Code #	Description	Fine
09-40-060	Park/Stand on Bicycle Path or Lane	$100.00
09-40-080	Parked/Standing Unattended Engine Running	$75.00
09-64-020(a)	Parallel Park more than 12" from Curb or in Wrong Direction	$25.00
09-64-020(b)	Stand or park to obstruct roadway (less than 18' of width on a two-way street or 10' on a one-way street	$75.00
09-64-020(c)	Motorcycle or Scooter not parked perpendicularly or diagonally	$25.00
09-64-030(b)	Park outside of diagonal markings	$50.00
09-64-040(b)	Park while street cleaning signs are posted and in effect.	$50.00
09-64-041	Park while special event signs are posted and in effect.	$60.00
09-64-0500)	Park in Disabled Parking space on street or in public or private lot	$200.00
09-64-060(b)	Park in Snow Route: 3-7 a.m.	$60.00
09-64-070	Park in Snow Route: More than 2" of snow.	$60.00
09-64-080(a)	Parking during Rush Hour	$60.00
09-64-080(b)	No Stand, Park Time Restricted	$60.00
09-64-090(e)	Park in violation of Residential Permit Parking (RPP) Zone	$60.00
09-64-091	Parking Without Industrial Parking Permit	$50.00
09-64-100(a)	Park within 15' of Fire Hydrant	$100.00

09-64-100(b)	Park In Fire Lane	$150 00
09-64-100(c)	Park as to block Access to/or efficient use of Alley, Driveway, or Fire Lane	$150.00
09-64-100(d)	Park as to block access to or use of Disabled Curb Cut	$75 00
09-64-100(e)	Park under Fire Escape	$100.00
09-64-100(f)	Park within 20' of Crosswalk where official signs are posted	$60.00
09-64-100(g)	Park within 30' of Stop Sign or Traffic Signal on approaching side	$60.00
09-64-100(h)	Park in front of Theater Entrance, Exit	$100.00
09-64-110(a)	Double Parking or Standing	$100.00
09-64-110(b)	Park or Stand within intersection, except for "T" Intersection	$75.00
09-64-110(c)	Park or Stand on Crosswalk	$60.00
09-64-110(d)	Park or Stand on Sidewalk	$60.00
09-64-110(e)	Park or Stand on Parkway, except in emergencies	$60.00
09-64-110(f)	Park or Stand on Bridge, except Stockton Drive	$75.00
09-64-110(g)	Park or Stand in Viaduct, Underpass	$75.00
09-64-110(h)	Park or Stand on or within 10' of Railroad Tracks	$100.00
09-64-120(a)	Park on City Property	$50.00
09-64-120(b)	Park or Stand on CHA Property	$50.00
09-64-130	Park or Block Alley	$150.00
09-64-140(b)	Park or Stand in Bus/Cab/Carriage Stand, except expeditious loading or unloading of passengers	$100.00
09-64-150(a)	Park or Stand near Fire Station or Railroad Crossing when signs posted	$100.00

09-64-150(b)	Parking or Standing Prohibited Anytime when signs posted	$60.00
09-64-160(b)	Park in Curb Loading Zone	$60.00
09-64-160(c)	Failure to possess or display Back-In Permit for loading	$60.00
09-64-170(a)	Park Truck, Recreation Vehicle more than 22 feet in length, Self-contained Motor Home, Bus, Taxi (except Wards 15 and 46), Livery Vehicle on a Residential Street. Note: Pickup trucks and vans are excepted in Wards 1, 9, 10, 12, 13, 14, 15, 16, 18, 19, 21, 22, 23, 26, 28, 29, 32, 33, 37, 40, 42, 43, 46, 49, and 50	$25.00
09-64-170(b)	Park Truck, Self-contained Motor Home, Bus on Business Street, except for expeditious loading or unloading	$25.00
09-64-170(c)	Stand/Park Vehicle 6' High or greater within 20' of crosswalk	$60.00
09-64-170(d)	Park Truck Tractor, Semitrailer, Commercial Truck, or Trailer on Business or Residential Street Except For Expeditious Loading or Unloading	$125.00
09-64-180(a)	Park in Loop 6:00 a.m. - 6:00 p.m. Monday through Friday, except holidays	$60.00
09-64-190	Expired Meter or Overstay Meter Period	$50.00
09-64-200(b)	Outside Metered Space as designated by pavement markings	$50.00
09-64-210	TV News Permit: Failure to Display or More than One Vehicle in Permit Area	$50.00
09-68-0400)	Park, Stand in violation of Wrigley Field Bus Permit Zone	$100.00
09-68-0400)	Privately Owned Bus: Motor Running in Wrigley Field Bus Permit Zone	$100.00
09-76-150(b)	Park with Burglar Alarm Sounding over Four Minutes	$25.00
09-80-080(a)	Park Vehicle to Display for Sale	$100.00

09-80-080(b)	Park to Grease or Repair, except for emergency	$100.00
09-80-080(c)	Park to Sell Merchandise	$100.00
09-80-110(a)	Abandoned Vehicle: 7 Days or Incapable of Operation	$75.00
09-80-110(b)	Hazardous Dilapidated Vehicle in public view (public or private property)	$75.00
09-80-120(a)	Not entitled to park in Public Lot	$50.00
09-80-120(b)	Not entitled to park in Private Lot	$25.00
09-80-130(a)	Park in City Lot: Failure to Pay or Outside designated Space	$50.00
09-80-130(b)	Park in City Lot: in facility After Hours	$50.00
09-80-130(c)	Park in City Lot: Over 30 Consecutive Days	$50.00

APPENDIX C

Compliance Violations

Code #	Description	Fine
09-40-170	Operation of Vehicle in Unsafe Condition	$25.00
09-40-220	Signal Required during operation	$25.00
09-64-125*	Failure to Display or Improper Display of City Sticker	$120.00
09-76-010(a)	Brakes required during operation	$25.00
09-76-010(b)	Motorcycle: Brakes required during operation	$25.00
09-76-010(c)	Trailer/Semitrailer: Brakes required during operation	$25.00
09-76-020(a)	Service Brakes: stopping capability during operation	$25.00
09-76-020(b)	Hand Brakes: stopping capability during operation	$25.00
09-76-020(c)	Service Brakes: stopping capability for Antique Vehicles during operation	$25.00
09-76-020(d)	Brakes Required during operation, Good Working Order	$25.00
09-76-030	Self-operating Windshield Wipers Required during operation	$25.00
09-76-040(a)	Horn Required during operation	$25.00
09-76-040(b)	Siren, Whistle, Bell Prohibited, except for emergency vehicle	$25.00
09-76-050(a)	Motorcycle: Exhibit Head Lamp visible for 500' during operation	$25.00
09-76-050(b)	Motor Vehicles: Two Head Lamps visible for 1000' during operation	$25.00
09-76-050(c)	Motor Vehicles: Red Rear Lamp visible for 500' during operation	$25.00

09-76-050(d)	Rear Plate Lighted and Legible for 50' during operation	$25.00
09-76-050(e)	Trailer: Two Red Rear Lamps visible for 500' during operation	$25.00
09-76-060(a)	Spot Lamps: More than One or Improperly Directed during operation	$25.00
09-76-060(b)	Auxiliary Driving Lamps: More than Three or Improperly Mounted during operation	$25.00
09-76-070(a)	Side Cowl or Fender Lamps: More than One per side or Emits Other than White or Amber Light during operation	$25.00
09-76-070(b)	Running Board Lamps: More than One per side or Emits Other than White or Amber Light during operation	$25.00
09-76-070(c)	Back-Up Lamp Continuously Lit during forward operation	$25.00
09-76-070(d)	More than Four Front Mounted Lamps during operation	$25.00
09-76-080	Non-motor vehicles Required Lighting: White Front Lamp visible for 500' or Red Rear Lamp visible for 500' during operation	$25.00
09-76-090(b)*	Required Lighting for vehicle parked on Unlit Street (1/2 hour after sunset or 1/2 hour before sunrise): White Front Lamp visible for 500' or Red Rear Lamp visible for 500'	$25.00
09-76-090(c)*	Lamps required to be Depressed or Dimmed while parked	$25.00
09-76-100(a)	Suspension Modified beyond 3" (body lifted from the chassis or variation in the horizontal line) when in operation, except motorcycles, motor-driven cycles, or off-highway racing vehicles	$25.00
09-76-110(a)	Bumpers: Front and Rear Required or Modified beyond 3" when in operation except motorcycles, motor-driven cycles, off-highway racing vehicles, or antique vehicles	$25.00
09-76-120	Rear View Mirror Required and located so as to reflect up to 200' during operation	$25.00

09-76-130	Trailer: Two Red Rear Reflectors Required , located 12" from lower left and right hand corners and visible form 300' during operation	$25.00
09-76-140(a)(1)	Muffler: Required or Not in Good Working Order during operation	$100.00
09-76-140(a)(2)	Muffler cutout, by-pass, or Straight Pipe during operation	$100.00
09-76-140(b)	Engine Required to Prevent Excessive Fumes or Smoke during operation	$25.00
09-76-160(a)*	Rear and Front Plates Required	$50.00
09-76-160(b)*	Rear Plate Required for Motorcycles, Trailers, Semitrailers	$50.00
09-76-160(c)*	Front Plate Required for Truck-Tractors	$50.00
09-76-160(d)*	Plates: Horizontal Positioning at Height of 12" Required, Visibility and Legibility Required, or Tinted Screens Prohibited	$50.00
09-76-160(f)*	Expired Plates or Temporary Registration	$50.00
09-76-170	Failure to display City Sticker during operation	$120.00
09-76-180(a)	Passenger Vehicles: Seat Safety Belts Required for drivers and front seat passengers during operation	$25.00
09-76-180(b)	School Bus: Seat Safety Belts Required for drivers and all passengers during operation	$25.00
09-76-190	Commercial or Industrial Enterprise Vehicles: Failure to Display Name, Address of Owner or Maximum Weight on both sides of vehicle during operation	$25.00
09-76-200(a)	Load Projects Beyond Line of the Fender on Left or 6' Beyond Line of the Fender on Right during operation	$25.00
09-76-200(b)	Load Projects Beyond 4' of Rear or vehicle's bed or body during operation, expect when a red lamp (at night) or cloth (at day) is displayed at extreme end of load	$25.00